MONEY DOESN'T SPEND ITSELF... SO, WHERE DID IT GO?

Simple Solution for Building a Solid Financial Foundation for Your Business

Janet Ickes

ISBN: 978-0-9894364-6-5

Library of Congress Control Number: 2020917397

Printed in Burlington, North Carolina USA by Excel With Me Press

For more information, visit www.JanetIckes.com.

The Difference

I got up early one morning and rushed right into the day.
I had so much to accomplish that I didn't have time to pray.
Problems just tumbled about me, and heavier came each task.

"Why doesn't God help me?" I wondered.
He answered, "You didn't ask."

I wanted to see joy and beauty, but the day toiled on, gray and bleak.
I wondered why God didn't show me.
He said, "But you didn't seek."

I tried to come into God's presence.
I used all my keys at the lock.
God gently and lovingly chided, "My child, you didn't knock."

I woke up early this morning and paused before entering the day.
I had so much to accomplish that I had to take time to pray.

Author: Unknown

Dedication

To my parents, whose love, support, and wisdom remain with me each and every day. I am so blessed to have such wonderful parents who provided me with an amazing foundation that I can share with those whom God places in my path; those who are willing to join me on this amazing journey called life.

Contents

A Special Bonus Gift from Janet

There's so much information out there about money management that can help you to run a profitable business, yet at the same time, it can be very confusing. When you finish this book, you'll be armed with what you need to know to build a foundation that will sustain future growth so that you can successfully manage your money. It's a great place to get started so that you can reduce hours researching, and instead focus more on what really matters.

As a special bonus for buying this book, I've created templates to help you get started with getting your arms around your business finances. It's the *Know Where Your Money Is Toolkit,* filled with downloadable templates to get you started tracking your income and expenses and creating a budget, as well as checklists to help you stay focused and on task with the key financial activities.

As an additional bonus, you'll also have access to a resource page with links to not only the resources mentioned in this book, but also to new tools, technologies, and programs I discover and recommend.

Just go to https://JanetIckes.com/MoneyToolKit
and let me know where to send your bonus kit.

As another special gift, I'll also be sending tips, tricks, and great information to make your life easier around your business finances.

Let's get started.

Janet

Introduction

Have you ever asked yourself, "Where did my money go?" If so, you are not alone.

Odds are, you have asked yourself this question more than once in your lifetime. Life has a funny way of getting us distracted from the things we need to be doing, especially when it comes to money.

- Do you know what your spending habits are?
- Do you buy it just because it's cool?
- Do you even consider if it's "in the budget?"

At some point in our lives, most of us will ask ourselves, "Where did my money go?" Most people buy things just because they want them without consideration of whether or not they can afford them. After all, it's America and "plastic" is a way of life. You can buy it now using your credit card and pay for it later. Only problem is when later arrives, your money seems to have spent itself.

Now, you must figure out how to pay that bill, which adds stress. When stress is added to your already busy life, you become more irritable; you don't sleep well; you are easily frustrated and angered with most people who cross your path. The next thing you know, your health deteriorates and your family suffers.

Since your personal and business lives mirror one another, the stress, the lack of sleep, and the frustration blend into chaos. This chaos makes you feel like you are running on a giant hamster wheel which goes faster and faster with no way to slow it down and get off. You are only able to focus on running and that is no way to live.

But wait, *Money Doesn't Spend Itself!* Money simply goes where you let it go. It's up to you to choose where your money goes, and you get to choose how you spend your money. You can choose to make better decisions. You can make some tough decisions today to build the foundation of success for tomorrow.

The only problem is where to start. There are so many systems out there and available to you, but with so many options it's easy to become overwhelmed. Especially since there is so little time to figure out which is best for you, let alone what may work for you. And when you are overwhelmed, often what ends up happening is you do nothing. But you don't need to be overwhelmed and do nothing because you can start with one step at a time.

The first step is to DECIDE to commit and act in a manner that will move you towards your financial goal. If you are willing to take the first step, this book is for you. Inside this book, you will be encouraged to ask yourself three key questions, questions you need to answer honestly. If you take responsibility for your choices and act accordingly so that you can figure out where your money went, you can not only bring it back, but start telling your money where to go.

Throughout the book, you will discover ways to find money that you didn't even realize you had. Implementing the strategies in response to the three main questions will help reduce the stress and the frustration around how to pay those bills. With less stress, you can begin to focus on both your professional and personal priorities and goals.

After leaving corporate America and moving to another state a few years ago, I realized that for my small business to replace my corporate career, I had to meet people. I didn't know anyone in this new state and if I was going to avoid going back to corporate America, I needed to build relationships; and what better way to do that than through networking? As I networked and started to build relationships, my small business grew.

However, I began to realize that one topic seemed to come up in these networking events that amazed me. One topic more than any other seemed to challenge many of the small business owners, entrepreneurs, and solopreneurs that I met. One topic raised so many challenges. One topic that, in my mind, was the foundation for any small business. But this one topic appeared to completely frustrate many of these proclaimed successful small business owners. What was that topic? MONEY! More specifically, the lack of money; the stress around money; the stress of not being able to pay themselves.

In a nutshell, the inability or lack of knowledge around how to manage money within their business.

It astounded me how often these small business owners, entrepreneurs, and solopreneurs, who believe they were successful, were unable to answer simple questions. Questions such as:

- What software or system do you use to track your income and expenses?
- What percentage of your income is your pay?
- How often do you pay yourself?

- What percentage of income do you set aside for taxes, insurance, equipment repairs and replacements?

Few were able to answer these questions, and most had no idea. How can you be in business and at the very least, not know when and how much you were getting paid?

This was sad, and it made me wonder where the confusion started and why so many of these owners were struggling. So, I asked, and I learned a few interesting things:

1. The way they manage their business finances was a direct reflection of how they managed their personal finances. All too often there was no money management on the personal level. Hmm… this may be part of the problem.
2. They realized that money management was important and a necessary process that they must undertake; however, it seemed overwhelming and they had no idea where to start. Therefore, they never started at all. Hmm… this may be another part of the problem.
3. Numbers are scary and confusing. Therefore, they were avoided. Hmm… now we are getting somewhere…

To me, numbers come easy. I thought it was simply part of life.

I soon realized that my "normal" was not so normal. Of course, normal is overrated in my opinion. Nonetheless, God has given each of us unique talents that we are to use for service to others. I was beginning to see how my journey was evolving and how I could make a real difference for those I meet. I was given the opportunity to blend my 20 years of corporate experience, my payroll and accounting skills along with my 17 years of small business experience, to help these small business owners and entrepreneurs implement and utilize simple systems to help them take control of their money. Systems that would help save time and increase profits.

Although it may not be easy, it is simple if you take one step at a time and build a solid foundation for long-term success and growth. And what was really interesting is that this same foundation works whether you are looking at your business or personal finances.

Stepping away from corporate America, moving to another state and downsizing to a one income family was an interesting journey. Moving costs, two house payments, two sets of utilities, etc. definitely made things challenging financially. However, 20 years of applying the strategies I'm sharing in this book made it possible to transition and build my small business in a new state without major stress and frustration. In fact, not only was I able to build my part-time business, I was blessed to begin a full-time entrepreneurial business alongside my part-time business. A business dedicated to igniting simple solutions to manage money. Whether it's for business or personal reasons, the foundation is the same. But it's up to YOU; m*oney doesn't spend itself.*

If you are looking for investment advice, this book is not for you. I leave investment advice to the experts who specialize in that area. They are the experts, so look to them for investment advice.

If you want me to tell you exactly **where** you should be spending your money, I cannot. This book does not offer suggestions for where to spend your money or how to prioritize your spending because it's up to you to decide based upon your priorities.

If you are looking for a guarantee for success, growth, and wealth, this book does not offer it. There are no guarantees in life.

However, it has been proven that through hard work, persistence, consistent effort, and the willingness to adapt as needed, success typically follows your efforts and you can build the foundation that supports growth and wealth.

Let me ask you a few questions:

- Do you spend more than you earn?
- Do you max out your credit cards because your bank account is zero?
- Would an emergency leave you financially devastated?
- Are you unable to pay yourself as the business owner?
- Do you feel like you are a hamster on a wheel when it comes to your finances and you have no idea how to make it stop or even slow down?
- Do you feel stressed and frustrated when bills are due because there is no money in your account?

If you answered "yes" to any of these questions, keep reading. This book is for you. It's work, it's tough, but it's possible. In fact, it's simple. Not easy, just simple.

One great side effect of this process is that both your business and personal finances will improve. Remember, personal and business money management mirror one another. The principles are the same, the foundation is the same, and the strategies are the same. And the best part of it all is that you can choose to take back control of your cash. Why? Because *money doesn't spend itself*. You get to decide where your money goes.

Are you ready to take the first step? Great. Continue reading, but more importantly, use the following pages of this book as a workbook to build a solid foundation. At the end of every chapter, you will see questions to reflect upon and pages to journal and capture your thoughts and key learnings. Action on your part is required, and it's the only way you can build this foundation which is vital to turning money into wealth, and it starts here. So, grab a pen and a highlighter and let's get started.

Remember, it's up to you. Money doesn't spend itself.

Chapter 1

Why am I Amazed and Confused?

"Money is only a tool. It will take you wherever you wish, but it will not replace you as the driver."

~Ayn Rand

Have you ever found yourself in a situation that totally confuses you? A situation that leaves you bewildered, surprised, or even amazed? Most would agree that at some point in their life, they have experienced a situation or two that fits this description. These situations come in many forms.

I attended a networking event where you could share information about yourself and your business. It always amazed me how successful all these business owners were, based on the successes they shared during their introductions. Yet on this particular occasion, I had the opportunity to join in on a conversation off in the corner.

One of my networking friends appeared visibly upset. Her head was down, her hand was on her forehead, and her shoulders were hunched. And when I approached her and she raised her head, I saw tears in her eyes. So I inquired if there was something that I could help her with. She admitted that she was extremely stressed. Both her income taxes and her insurance payments were due the next week and there was not enough money in her bank account to make both payments. In fact, the more we talked, the more I learned. And the more amazed I became.

Every time this situation occurred, and both her taxes and insurance were due, which was the case approximately every three months, my friend had the same reaction. She was stressed because the money was not in her account. As we talked more, I learned that she had not taken a paycheck from her business in the last six months. What? No paycheck for six months? No wonder my friend was upset.

Money, especially the lack of, causes a lot of stress. At the same time, I was bewildered. Although I didn't say it out loud, I could hear myself asking, "Why are you in business if you cannot pay yourself?" This entire situation felt very odd to me, as I was very blessed to have been taught to prepare for upcoming expenses. I was taught early about how to build a solid foundation when it came to money.

My dad was a stickler when it came to money. In fact, when I wanted to get my first car, I had to prove to him, in "black and white," that I could afford this car. So, I created a spreadsheet that showed my income and my expenses (limited as they were) to prove to him that I could afford it. My mom tried to warn me before talking to Dad that I had to be prepared because "you know your father." I handed her the printout. Her response was simply – "I should have known; you are just like your father."

The more I talked with folks, the more I realized that few of my fellow networkers had a solid money foundation in their early years. Few were taught from the beginning to set aside money for a rainy day. In fact, very few even knew what a rainy-day fund meant. I began to realize that my situation was not the normal, rather the normal for most was quite the contrary. This amazed me.

The foundation that I was given unfolded even in my Mary Kay business. My Mary Kay training taught me to use a 60/40 rule when it came to money management. To be successful and run a profitable business, it was recommended as income came in, you should set aside 60% of it to replace inventory, using the remaining 40% to cover everything else, including your paycheck. Having that solid foundation, I simply followed what was recommended. As the income came in from my sales, I set aside 60% to replace my inventory. And I knew exactly how much money I had to work with when it came to re-ordering my inventory.

Come to think of it, many of my Mary Kay sisters experienced a similar reaction. Because I was proactive and followed the system, I was not tempted to over order inventory as many of my sister consultants did. Often, they would look at their bank balance and decide based upon the amount in their account what they could spend whether it was for inventory or something that they wanted. They "forgot" that unless they set money aside, not all that money was "available" to spend. In fact, in many cases, the money was already spent on expenses like insurance, taxes, and necessary supplies for the skin care classes. The credit card bill had not come in yet.

Frustration was common until they began to use the training taught. Over the years, I was able to share my process with my Mary Kay sisters and team members. And I was realizing that the same process and a similar system could be adapted and implemented for my fellow business owners. A simple process that if used, could reduce the stress associated with money, especially the lack of it when known, inevitable expenses were due.

I could utilize the same process I did with my part-time business. The concept would work, as my yearly trips illustrated. By following the sales and marketing processes, I generated income so that I received a monthly paycheck from my Mary Kay business. So, I set aside my paycheck (which was a portion of that 40%) in a separate account. Then, I would use my paycheck to cover my yearly trip to our Mary Kay conference in Dallas. The best part was that not only did my paycheck cover my expenses for the trip, it also covered the expenses for both my husband and son to join me. We enjoyed a mini family vacation each year. In fact, one year, we extended our Dallas trip to include an additional week and headed to Sea World and Six Flags. That solid foundation made it possible for us to get away as a family each year without the stress of wondering if the money would be available.

There is hope. Yes, owning a business full-time is stressful. But stress from not knowing how your money is coming in and out of your business should not be. Yet, for most it was. Numbers in general were confusing and frustrating. And this astounded me because I knew that it didn't have to be so stressful and confusing. Building a solid foundation and incorporating the tools and strategies that I personally and professionally used would reduce the stress that many of my fellow networkers experienced.

The more I listened, the more I realized that what appeared to be the case may not really be the case, especially for many small business owners. Over the past several years, prior to the pandemic crisis in early 2020, it appeared that businesses had grown, unemployment was down, consumer confidence was up, and the economy was improving. Overall, it appeared that most businesses were doing better than they ever had.

If this is the case, how could so many small businesses run without sound money management practices in place?

Why do many of these small business owners not take home a paycheck?

How can these owners deem their business successful if they don't pay themselves?

Isn't the primary reason that most decide to become an entrepreneur to make money themselves instead of relying on someone else? Why else would you be in business? It would be better to get a job and maintain an expensive hobby. At least you would have a paycheck to live on. I found this whole real-world reality absolutely astounding.

Starting and running a business is difficult. The life of an entrepreneur is challenging but can be extremely rewarding as well. To untangle the truths about entrepreneurial life, I knew I had to begin to make connections, to talk with more people. Listen to their challenges. For I knew that I would face these same challenges as I transitioned from having a full-time corporate career to being a full-time entrepreneur. And there is no better way to make connections and build relationships than networking.

Amazing Networking Discoveries

"The richest people in the world look for and build networks, everyone else looks for work."

~Robert Kiyosaki

Networking is one of the many opportunities to get out and meet new friends, build relationships, and connect with other small business owners. As a new resident in a new state where my family did not know anyone, networking was a blessing as it made it possible for me to meet new people right away, people who were entrepreneurs and who had strengths that complemented mine.

I found myself in an interesting situation when we first moved. One that, if I was honest, made me understand all too well what my friend was experiencing. Due to the move, we found ourselves reduced to a one income family, something that we had not been for over 20 years. Yes, it was by design and I looked at it as a fresh opportunity to grow my Mary Kay business into a full-time one.

The only problem, which I thought I had planned for, proved to be a little more challenging than expected. We had moving costs, along with duplicate house expenses since our first home had not sold yet. In addition, we had to get the new house set up, which I found would include many expenses that I did not consider, such as the multiple trips between states to get everything moved. All these unexpected expenses added up quickly. It was exhausting and exciting at the same time. And I was so looking forward to becoming a full-time entrepreneur which this move made possible.

The first couple of months I was prepared for. I had saved, so we were in good shape, right? At the six-month point, our first house still had not sold. Those duplicate expenses drained what I had put back and after the first few months, I was forced to dip into our savings heavily. Thankfully, I had saved for 20 years, so at least there was a savings account to work with.

During this time, my business was growing, but slower than I had hoped. Sales were coming in, but my team was not growing as I needed. It was going to take the combination of sales and team in order to provide the income needed to sustain our lifestyle, especially if we wanted to eat. Otherwise, I was going to have to go back to a corporate job to make the bills. This was not the direction I wanted to go in at all.

Our savings account was dwindling fast. Stress increased tremendously as I just didn't know how we were going to pay all the bills. But I had a foundation in place and that foundation sustained us for those six months. Miraculously, at the end of six months, at the point where I had no choice but to say, "Lord, it's in your hands," we got the call that our home had sold. We didn't get what we asked, but it sold. The duplicate bills would finally stop. Know what was really interesting? The amount we received for the sale of our home allowed me to pay off the few remaining loans so that we only had our house payment to deal with. We could get back on track. We could start rebuilding our savings account, one step at a time.

Now that I had all these extra hours, I knew that I needed to grow my business faster. Since our plan eliminated my career in corporate America, I had an extra 60 hours a week to work with. Lots of hours available to network now that we were back on track and I wasn't so stressed out.

Of course, to grow that business, I had one major challenge: I needed to meet a lot more people. My business is based on clients who have tried and liked our skin care and color products. In addition, they choose to partner with me as their consultant. But I still had to meet them – and what better way than networking?

So that's what I did.

Meeting people became easy now that I was networking regularly and not so stressed. It was amazing how much more I smiled, now capable of building those relationships without the constant stress.

There were lots of networking opportunities. Whether it was Monday, Tuesday, Wednesday, Thursday, or Friday, there were networking events that you could choose to visit. Some were free to attend; others had a cost. Networking allows you to meet people, make connections, and build relationships. What more could you want? Business is going to be a success. Right?

Yes, I was able to grow and build my business and form many new relationships. But as I was networking, I became aware of a common concern among my networking friends. That stress was revealed over and over. And when I really listened, many of the small business owners boasted of a six-figure business and how successful they were. During the time to share they highlighted the best of their business. They smiled while talking about their business and shared how great it was to be a small business owner, entrepreneur, or solopreneur. They were excited to share how they were running a successful business. Yet at the same time, I began to really notice that many were also stressed because next week's bills were due, and they were struggling to pay. There were two sides to networking. One side highlighted the best, and one, if you really listened, proved to be quite the opposite of successful.

At first, I never heard mention of the challenges, the difficulties associated with owning your own business. It was not until I really learned to listen and open up about my own struggles that I realized that many small business owners struggled with money management. The same issues facing my Mary Kay sisters were facing my fellow entrepreneurs. The same challenges and stress I faced were all too common for many whom I began to build relationships with.

Over and I over I would hear the same reaction, especially when it came to paying taxes. First, it appeared that most seemed surprised by income tax. That was a little confusing to me. In my world, taxes are expected. One thing you know for sure is that you will pay taxes when it comes to your business, at least if you are profitable and making money. You can rest assured that the government expects to be paid and will rarely accept the excuse that "you didn't know" you owed taxes. I was amazed to find that so many of these business owners were surprised that the government expects them to pay their taxes.

Of course, that tax payment is based on profits from your business, based on whether or not your successful business made money. Think about it: If you were not expected to pay taxes, then that means you didn't make any money. You were not profitable. I understand you may not like to pay taxes, but if you are not required to pay taxes from your income received, then you won't have to worry about it very long because you will be out of business. You can then get a job working for someone else and not worry about those unexpected business tax payments because it will be someone else's problem.

In the corner, truths were revealed. Truths that these situations were a much bigger dilemma than I realized.

Here's what I know:

- If you are unable to take a paycheck from your business, it means you are not paying your bills, unless you have another income source outside of your business.
- If you are not taking a paycheck, not paying your bills, or subsidizing your business by other means, it probably means that you are fooling yourself about how successful your business is.
- If you are unable to take a paycheck, you are most likely in denial as to just how profitable your business is. And if you think about it, you must begin to question whether you are even profitable at all.

It baffled me how some businesses that brought in $10,000 were more profitable than those businesses making $500,000 a year in revenue. The bottom line is that, whether it's admitted or not, without profits, long-term business success is impossible.

How can you own a business, claim that your business is successful, yet your business doesn't provide you a paycheck? I simply find that amazing. Don't you? Especially since money doesn't spend itself.

There is an Elephant in the Room

"When there is an elephant in the room introduce him."

~ Randy Pausch

As I uncovered these truths from networking, I began to understand that there was really "an elephant in the room" that many small business owners chose to ignore or at least tried to. You know that "elephant" or obvious problem or difficult situation that people do not want to talk about. The more I talked with folks, the more I understood, the more I realized, that for many, *money management* was the elephant in the room.

As I talked with more small business owners, I became even more astounded to learn just how big this elephant, or money problem, was for many of these people.

Typical questions like:

- Where do you spend your money?
- How much money was invested in areas such as product development, customer acquisition, marketing and messaging, or administrative costs?

earned the response, "I don't know."

These are all the places your money has to go to run a successful and profitable business.

The responses, "I just kind of pay the bills," or "That's just how it works; the loudest one gets paid first," or "The squeaky wheel gets the grease," simply surprise me.

How can you run your business or call yourself a successful business owner if you just pay the squeaky wheel? It makes no sense. That's definitely not how truly successful business owners operate.

There is so much stress associated with only paying the overdue bills with collection calls coming in. There is so much frustration associated with only paying the bills based on which collections person yells the loudest for payment.

What's so confusing to me is that it doesn't have to be this stressful. If you are willing to take control of your money and manage your money, you can reduce your stress and frustration levels. You can actually be prepared for upcoming taxes and other payments.

There was an elephant in the room that needed to be revealed. And there has to be a way to start talking about money, so that others are inspired to take control of their money. A way to ignite the possibilities that are available for both your personal and business finances. And there is a way. A simple, not necessarily easy, way to introduce this elephant named "Money." Why? Because *money doesn't spend itself.*

When in doubt, Google

"Research is formalized curiosity. It is poking and prying with a purpose."

~Zora Neale Hurston

What do you do when you are not sure about something and you would like to understand why things are the way they are? You do what most of us do. You Google it. Or you can ask Siri or Alexa. Of course, you may learn a few things you didn't expect. But all in all, there is a wealth of information available to reduce your curiosity about what you hear. Because I was so amazed and astounded at I what I learned through networking, I decided to do a little research. You know what I found out?

Small Businesses…

- In five years, over half of small businesses will close. Why? The number one reason was the inability to manage their cash flow. In fact, 82% of small businesses admitted they failed due to the inability to manage their cash flow. 82%! That means if we are in a room of 100, only 18 are going to make it

Money Factoid: 82% of small business failure is due to inability to manage cash flow [1].
~Source: US Bank Study

Most Americans…

- Two-thirds of Americans would struggle to scrounge up $1000 in an emergency[2]. ~The Associated Press
- Nearly one-third of Americans pay the minimum due on their credit cards each month, which led to an average of

$600,000 paid in interest alone[3]. ~FINRA's National Financial Capability Study

- Total Outstanding US Consumer Debt: $3.9 trillion[4]. ~ Survey of Consumer Finances by the U.S. Federal Reserve

Money Factoid: Two-Thirds of Americans would struggle to scrounge up $1,000 in an emergency ~The Associated Press

I thought it may have been me and that this money management issue was not really that big of a deal. Maybe I was just talking to the wrong people. Not so. Research indicates that this is even a bigger challenge for people, on both the business and personal levels.

Digging a little deeper, talking with even more folks, I began to discover that often the elephant (money) was often fed by the lack of details. Details such as:

- The actual amount of income and expenses attributed to each month.
- The exact amount of transactions that flow in and out of your account.
- The total income and expenses for each month, each quarter, each year.

These key details let you compare one month to another. They allow you to discover trends (both good and bad within your finances) so that you make better decisions. They create the required reports to analyze income and expenses over periods of time. Without these details, you cannot make good decisions in your personal and business lives.

You need these details to make better financial decisions based on facts rather than emotions or pure guesswork. Without these key details, it would explain why only 18 out of 100 businesses were successful and two-thirds of Americans struggled to find $1,000 in the light of an emergency.

Is it the forest or the trees?

"When you pay attention to detail, the big picture will take care of itself."

~ George St-Pierre

Unless...

"You can't see the forest for the trees."

~John Heywood

Successful businesses are able to see the details of their finances, to analyze reports, and use those details to make smarter decisions when it comes to managing their money. Hugely successful business owners have a healthy relationship with money and view it as a trusted tool for success.

Would you agree that to have a solid financial foundation, you must have the details of exactly where your money goes? Without the details, you cannot see the big picture. However, if you focus on too many details, you won't be able to see the big picture.

On one hand, you need a big picture to focus on, so that you can make wise decisions that will lead you toward your ultimate goal of running a successful business that provides a paycheck to support your personal life.

On the other hand, you must focus on the all the details to be able to reveal the big picture. What a dilemma.

Trying to look at all the details so you can clearly see the big picture can completely overwhelm you to the point that you end up confused, frustrated, and stressed. You simply can't see the forest from the trees.

There is so much confusion around money management. The confusion leads to stress, and before long, stress is controlling both your business and personal life. Considering that your money habits from your personal life tend to mirror your business life, often both are a mess. If you struggle with your personal finances, you will struggle in your business finances. Yes, it's a dilemma. Details regarding money are essential and overwhelming at the same time.

So why expend the time and energy to get your arms around your numbers so you can be in control of your finances? If you want to be a successful business owner, it's required. There is no way around it.

Here's the great news. There is a simple solution that together we can create and implement that will eliminate this dilemma, one that provides a way to track the details and summarize those details in a format that will help you work smarter, not harder!

It's Time to Work Smarter, Not Harder!
Money doesn't spend itself!

You can choose wisely, or not

Therefore, everyone who hears these words of mine and puts them into practice is like a wise man who built his house upon the rock. The rain came down, the streams rose, and the winds blew and beat against the house, yet it did not fall, because it had its foundation on the rock.

~ Matthew 7:24-25 (NIV)

By now, I suspect you would agree that figuring out how to deal with money proves quite the dilemma for many people. Just like a hamster on a wheel, you are running around in circles with no end in sight. You are spinning around and around until exhaustion makes the wheel stop, one way or another.

You have a choice on what foundation you build on. In the Bible, the parable of the wise man and foolish man teaches us the importance of building on a solid foundation of rock. If you want to weather the storms, the challenges, the stress, the frustration, you must build your foundation on solid rock. You must build a system that will provide the details for that foundation so that it will support your financial needs. You can choose to be like the wise man and build your foundation on solid rock.

Whereas the wise man built upon rock, the foolish man built his house upon the sand. So, when the rain came down, the streams rose, and the winds blew and beat against the house, it fell with a great crash.

~ Matthew 7: 27 (NIV)

Or you can choose to build your foundation on sand. Sand will not withstand the storms that you will face; it will not withstand the stress and frustration. Your house will fall; your business will fail. Too many build their money foundation on sand, which would explain why over 50% of businesses fail within the first five years.

Money Factoid: Over 50% of small businesses fail within the first five years[5]. Source: Bureau of Labor Statistics

It may also explain why too many have personal finances in shambles. This is why a $400 charge causes panic for most Americans[6]. Yet, the choice is yours. You can build your foundation on rock or on sand. One is a wise choice: one a foolish choice. But it is a choice. Your choice. Remember, *money doesn't spend itself.*

Money doesn't spend itself

"Your life is a result of the choices you have made. If you don't like your life, start making better choices."

~ Zig Ziglar

Although I am amazed and astounded, I quickly realized that there is a solution. Money did not have to be such a major challenge for folks in their personal or business lives.

Business in general is simple. I will confess that I don't know everything there is to know about business. But I do know that in order to have a successful business, one that supports your personal lifestyle with a regular paycheck, you must serve enough people and know the cost of serving those people, so that you have a profit at the end of the day and can pay yourself.

It's fairly simple. When you have a profit, you make money. When you make money, you can pay employees. And by the way, if you are a small business owner, entrepreneur, or solopreneur, YOU are the employee. And you are in business to get paid.

I realize this is a simple way to look at business. Business **is** simple. Note, I said simple, not easy. Odds are when you started your business, you knew you could solve a problem for someone else. You had a solution to their problem.

That solution has a cost. But at the end of the day, you must make enough money over and above that cost to make a profit so that you can get paid. Otherwise why are you in business?

If your goal is to have an expensive hobby, don't concern yourself with making a profit. Either way is fine, but just be truthful to yourself as to whether you are in business or running an expensive hobby.

The more people I spoke to, the more I heard the same story over and over and over. So much that I began to get frustrated and then I just became sad. Sad because I don't think anyone ever said, "I am going to start a business, call it successful, and not have any money."

The truth is, when you own a business that doesn't make money and you have no idea how you are going to pay your bills, you become stressed. When you are stressed, it's tough to focus. When you are stressed, you go home stressed, you don't sleep well, you don't eat well, you yell at your kids, you yell at your spouse, and you cut yourself off from friendships. Your only focus is on how to survive, and that's no way to live.

It saddened me to know that so many of those whom I met were stressed and frustrated regarding money management. This stress and frustration often created the inability to implement solid money management practices. Too many were confused by the numbers. Too many were overwhelmed by the details. Too many were unsure what to do or where to start.

I began to realize that there was another part to my entrepreneurial journey that was unfolding as I was growing my Mary Kay business, something that brought my passion for teaching and educating to the foreground. I know money management does not have to be complicated. It's totally possible to build a solid foundation. I had done it for years. My foundation sustained us during a very stressful time.

I had shared my strategies and helped others in the past, especially when it came to money management. Was I being called to do it again, this time with a focus on the small business owners I had been networking with over the past year and built relationships with? The answer was becoming clear.

Yes, this was something that I was being called to do.

My passion for training and to find ways to streamline processes was ignited. Possibilities began to emerge, and I began to share with others how to implement a simple system that tracks their income and expenses, provides the reporting necessary to make good financial decisions, and builds a foundation on solid rock.

Together, we can discover ways to work smarter, not harder. Together we can break through these challenges and excel. There is a basic solution that involves a little addition and subtraction along with either pen and paper or computer software. You have a choice.

You decide the system to track the details of your money, not whether you are going to manage your money. What would it be like to not feel stressed? To know you can pay those bills? To know what those bills are before they are due? To pay yourself from your business?

What's even better is what reducing the stress around money management does for your life, your family, and your health.

What would it feel like to enjoy the freedom associated with owning your own business?

What would it feel like to know that you are able to pay your bills with the money in your account?

Is it just a dream? If so, let this dream become the incentive to work towards taking the actions needed to manage your money. Imagine how it would feel to know that you are able to pay your bills without stress.

What would it feel like to reduce your stress levels when it's time to pay your bills?

What would it feel like for you to enjoy the financial freedom from a profitable small business?

How would you feel? Would your health improve? Would your family life improve?

Let me ask you:

- Are you ready and willing to take the next step?
- Are you willing to honestly answer three simple questions to enable you to build your solid financial foundation on rock?
- Are you ready to improve both your personal and business life?
- Are you ready to reduce the stress when it comes to money?

Isn't it time to manage your money instead of letting your money manage you?

We will start with a few simple questions that, if you answer with honesty, will guide you as you build your foundation. As you reflect on your answers, you will find solutions, areas for improvement, and areas of strength. All will start to be revealed as you work through this book.

And by the time we get through exploring the final question, you will have a system that you can start using now to build a foundation to manage your money. You will have a system that will move you towards a streamlined process that will support your growth. You will have knowledge of options available to make things simpler. And you will have a resource available to support you.

Remember, your personal and business money management styles mirror one another. It's a package deal. The solution is simple, not easy. But I can assure you it is well worth it.

So, let's start by reflecting where you are right now. Answer the following questions honestly and discover where you are. Once we have the starting point, we can work towards moving to where you want to be. It's your choice. We will take one step at a time. After all, money doesn't spend itself.

Remember, it's up to you. Money doesn't spend itself.

A Time to Reflect

1. Does your business provide you a paycheck?

   ❐ Yes

   ❐ No

2. Do you have a system in place to track your money?

   ❐ Yes

   ❐ No

3. Do you pay bills on time, without stress?

   ❐ Yes

   ❐ No

4. Do you know the amount of your bills before they arrive and when they are due?

   ❐ Yes

   ❐ No

5. Do you know what your top five expenses are?

   ❐ Yes

   ❐ No

~if you answered "Yes" to all the above, you are well on your way to building your "money foundation on solid rock." If not… it's time to shift from building on sand to building on rock.

Inspirational Thought:

For I know the plans I have for you, declares the Lord, plans to prosper you, and not to harm you; plans to give you hope and a future. ~ Jeremiah 29:11 (NIV)

Reflection Journal

✓ Monthly paycheck

- *My ideal pay each month is*______________________
- *What I pay myself each month*___________________

  (You may average the last six months for this exercise)
- *What is the difference?* ________________ *(subtract ideal minus pay)*

✓ Money System

- *How do I track my income/expenses? (check one)*
  - ★ *I don't*
  - ★ *pen and paper*
  - ★ *computer software*
- *Is my system efficient?* _______________*(yes/no)*
- *Am I willing to explore an alternative?* _______*(yes/no)*
- *How important to me is having an effective money management system in place?* ______________
  - ★ *On scale 1-10; 1-not important; 10-very important*

✓ Personal / Business – *are a mirror of one another, but…*

- *Are my business and personal bank accounts and credit cards separate?* ____________*(yes/no)*

Reflection Summary

# of Yes answers from questions 1-5: ______________

~If you answered more "Yes" than "No" for questions 1-5, you are beginning to build your money foundation on rock.

Difference between ideal pay and actual pay ________

~If your number is positive, you are building on rock; if it's negative, you are building on sand.

How important is having an efficient money management system to you? ____________________________

~if it's below 7, you may want to make plans to get a job. If it's over 7, I will help you build your foundation on rock. Keep reading and working through this book.

Are your business and personal accounts separate? _____

~if not, open another account and separate them. This is step one.

Remember, it's up to you. Money doesn't spend itself.

Notes/Thoughts

Chapter 2

Where Is My Money? It's Not In My Account

"Don't tell me where your priorities are. Show me where you spend your money and I'll tell you what they are."

~James W. Frick

Seeing the shortest line at the grocery store, I rush over to get in line. As soon as I step into the line, I realize quickly why it is the shortest line. The lady in front of me has a cart filled to the brim. I have a choice here: I could roll my eyes and let stress take over or I could smile and make the best of the situation. I decide to make the best of this situation. After all, I do have a choice. I thought to myself that I may as well make a new friend since we're going to be here a while.

I soon notice that she has three big bags of dog food in her cart. So, I ask her what kind of dogs she has. She responds, "A chihuahua." (My mind races in disbelief. A chihuahua, seriously; three big bags of dog food for a chihuahua, but then I recall my decision to make the best of this and make a new friend.) So, I politely comment, "He must really like that food."

Her response? "Oh no, he likes canned food. But the dry food was on sale." WHAT?! I was speechless.

Can you relate? How often do you make decisions, just like this woman?

- It's on sale, so I'll just pick it up.
- I'm saving money, so I need to buy it today.
- It's new, and I just have to have it.

How often do you just say "yes" before you decide whether it's needed, if you really want it, or whether you can afford it? Of course, plastic is an option. You can put it on the credit card and pay the bill later. That's how it works in America!

The only problem is when it's time to pay the credit card bill, reality sets in, then stress shows up, and finally frustration takes over because, for some reason, you owe more than is available in your bank account. Now what? What are you going to do? Pay the minimum amount due on your bill or not pay the bill at all?

Too often these "squirrel moments" catch many people off guard. You make purchases without thinking, without really deciding whether you really need it; without considering if you can afford it. The credit card is right there in your wallet and so easy to pull out to pay for this great item. Consider comedian Steve Martin's comment about money:

> *"I love money. I love everything about it. I bought some pretty good stuff. Got me a $300 pair of socks. Got a fur sink. An electric dog polisher. A gasoline powered turtleneck sweater. And, of course, I bought some dumb stuff, too. "*
>
> ~ Steve Martin

Have you ever found yourself in a similar situation where you may have bought some dumb stuff too? I'm guessing that you may have once or twice, or you at least know someone who has. It's easy to say "yes" in the moment and not make the right choice. How often do you make payments on something and you don't even know where it is? You put it on your credit card because you just had to have it. Then in two years when you need it, you go out and buy it again.

Question 1: Where is my money?

"We are what we repeatedly do. Excellence, then, is not an act, but a habit. "

~ Aristotle

Understanding your spending habits is a great way to begin figuring out where your money is going so that you can take control of your money. Typically, spending habits fall on one end of the spectrum or another; either you are considered a spender or a saver. Both have benefits, and a blend of the two habits tends to be the best option for long-term success. And in many cases, you will find a little of both in you. But more than likely, you will favor one way or the other.

Consider how you would respond to the following questions:

1. Do you have money left over after paying your bills_each month?
2. Are you afraid to spend money?
3. Do you stick to a budget?
4. Do you pay your bills on time every month?
5. Do you have a savings and retirement account?

If you answered "yes" to most of these questions, that means you are a saver. If you answered "no" to most of these questions, that means you are a spender.

There are pros and cons to each type of habit. Typically, if you are a saver, you are a planner. You find it easier to save money, operate on a budget, and pay your bills early or on time, and you spend sparingly. And in many instances, this is a good thing. However, as a saver, you often experience more anxiety around finances, and you take fewer risks when investing and thus potentially receive less rewards. And if you are not willing to invest money or use it to gain assets and more education, opportunities can be lost. On the other side, if you are a spender, you are most likely less detailed. You are more willing to purchase and buy things quickly. You often fail to plan for long-term financial goals and credit card debt. However, your willingness to take more risks in the moment when investing may provide greater rewards.

Responses – When It Comes To Money

Understanding your tendency and responses when it comes to money is beneficial so that you can make better decisions. Knowledge is power. You may or may not identify with one of the responses below. That's ok. Understanding the responses is the key. There are strengths and weaknesses to both sides of these responses. Understanding will not only help you identify where your strengths lie but may clue you in to a few weaknesses as well.

Understanding both strengths and weaknesses in your own personal money response will only encourage improvement.

The Teenager's Response

"Don't buy things you can't afford with money you don't have to impress people you don't like."

~ Dave Ramsey

For those of you who have been blessed to live with a teenager, or spent time around a typical teen, I suspect that you have found some common responses when it comes to money. In fact, parents of teens often share similar experiences when it comes to their teen's response to money, especially when that teenager recently obtained driving privileges.

It is amazing how these new teenage drivers tend to believe that they are now adults, and so, should obtain all those great things that they believe adults have, such as a car, spending money, new computer games, a new computer, or the newest smartphone. It's even more surprising that somehow in the teen's mind, the car that they are now able to drive can somehow magically drive itself without the need to purchase gas or required maintenance related to wear and tear. And certainly, there was no reason to plan for such expenses; the car was magical.

In fact, it seems that most teens also believe that money miraculously finds its way into their pocket whenever there is a need. And if for some reason, their pocket remains empty, there is no hesitation to ask Mom or Dad for a couple of bucks so they can go out with their friends. After all, it's only 20 bucks…today, tomorrow, next Friday, and next Saturday.

I found this response interesting. What was also fascinating from the teen's response was that there seemed to be a money tree in the backyard; a money tree that provided cash for all these things that the teen expected. Rarely was there consideration or thought given to how much the teen spent over a week, a month, or a year. There was no need to worry about such things since there was a magical tree in the backyard. It was really interesting to observe how teens could enjoy the food that just appeared on the dinner table every night, how the lights turned on at the flip of a switch, and how their phones, which typically cost more than a computer, just automatically connected to this cool thing called the internet so that they could keep in constant contact with their friends. It must be the money tree.

It is amazing how this money tree also provided new clothes, especially when last year's pants become capris or even shorts. It's amazing how the insurance premium didn't increase that much when they were added to the insurance policy. Well, not that much anyway; it was just a few extra dollars here and there. The money tree could handle it.

More often than not, teenagers think nothing of spending now and paying later. They get what they want in the moment they want it. There is no thought to the actual total amount of money spent daily for these little things. They believe that it's just a couple of dollars, which really doesn't add up to much.

If you are around a teen, I know that you have experienced this response. In fact, if you are willing to be honest, I suspect you know an adult who shares this same response. Maybe even you. Can you relate to this response? The response to just spend now when you want it and pay for it later?

You know who you are; you are like the lady in the grocery store. It's on sale so I am just going to get it. You see this really cool item on Amazon that you just have to have. And it's really easy to buy it. You just need to click here and it's on its way to your house. In fact, that really cool item is often delivered directly to your doorstep within two days. It's magic. There is no cash required. You just buy it now and pay for it later. It's the American Way!

You don't agree? Considering that over 50% of Americans spend more than they make, I know that at least half of you, if you were willing to be honest, know this is true.

MONEY FACTOID: Over 50% of Americans spend more than they make[7]. Source: Association of Young Americans (AYA) and AARP

In fact, I would bet that at some point, we have all had this response. I know I have. There are times when you really want something and you give in to the "buy now, pay later" response. You are human, after all, and so many believe that it's just fine to always respond this way. And if you have a system in place, you may be able to respond this way on occasion. However, if you don't have a system in place that allows you to realize how you make purchase decisions, this response causes a tremendous amount of stress when the bill is due.

Could it be that this teenage type of response contributes to the stress associated with money among my networking friends? The more I talked to small business owners, the more I began to understand that many share the "buy now, pay later" response. Many small business owners thought nothing of buying it now just because it was new and the latest and greatest thing. It didn't matter that they had bought the latest and greatest every Friday for the past 12 weeks.

What was even more fascinating was how often the really cool item was never used or used once or twice. How often is that really cool item misplaced after two weeks? How often could have used the really cool item in the past six months, but you forgot where it was and decided to buy a new one instead?

In reality, I would suspect that most have a little teenager response time to time when it comes to buying things. You now realize that the "buy it now, pay for it later" response can cause a great deal of stress. This stress increases dramatically when you have no idea if the money needed to pay the bill is in your account.

And that is the key: Do you know that the money is in your account? If you know you favor this response, why not implement a system to minimize the stress caused? Let me suggest this option. Start setting aside a little bit of money each paycheck in a separate account. It may only be a couple dollars here and there depending on your situation. Then when you get that urge to respond with the "buy now, pay later" response, do one thing first. Check the balance in that account. If the money is there, make the purchase. Now the hard part comes into play: make no additional purchases on impulse until that bill is paid.

Spending without consideration of the true balance available (which is not typically your checking account balance) leads to the inability to have money to pay your bills that you have already committed to. If there is no money in your account, you cannot pay your contractors or employees, and you surely can't pay yourself. Now you feel that you are working for nothing. And the truth is that you are right. The feeling that you are back on a hamster wheel going faster every minute is very real and there is no way to slow it down, let alone stop it and step off. So why not do something about it?

The Investor's Response

> *"The best investment you can make, is an investment in yourself… the more you learn, the more you will earn."*
>
> ~Warren Buffet

In contrast, if you are able to apply the principles in this book, you can figure out a way to save a little money so that you have an opportunity to, once in a while, purchase with the "buy now, pay later" philosophy. Better yet, you can exchange money for a long-term benefit to strengthen your foundation. One of the best investments you can make regarding your money is to invest in yourself. Invest in education and in personal and professional development. Invest and learn from experts how you can better manage money. When you invest, you begin to slow that hamster wheel. You begin to understand the importance of money and you are able to start controlling your money.

When you are willing to invest in yourself and your team, you can exchange money for systems that identify where your money is going, which will lead to better decisions and reduce unnecessary spending. Of course, you have to be disciplined enough to set aside some money when it comes in to be able to invest in yourself. The value gained by investing in the education and systems to begin to understand and control your money will far outweigh the cost in the long run. You will become a greater, more efficient asset to your business. This efficiency will then allow you to get more results at a lower cost per result.

The Giver's Response

In everything I did, I showed you that by this kind of hard work we must help the weak, remembering the words the Lord Jesus himself said: "It is more blessed to give than to receive."

Acts 20:35 (NIV)

According to the Bible, it is better to give than to receive. These are great words to live by. Most of us would agree it's often a surprise blessing that means more than anything, especially when you receive that blessing when least expected, in times of greatest need.

When you begin to invest in yourself to take control of your money, you can be a giver without concerning yourself with **how** you will be able to give. It is part of how you operate and your normal day-to-day response. Part of a business's long-term success, believe it or not, is the willingness and ability to give. Incorporating a giver response may not seem like it will work, yet if you are willing to be honest, most would have to agree that we do indeed "reap what we sow." Most of you, if you are honest, can recall a time when it seemed that giving made no logical sense. Yet somehow, when you were willing to give in faith, to your amazement, you received an unexpected blessing.

What would it be like to be able to have a system in place that made giving simple? To give when you felt led without thought as to the how? You know it's better to give than to receive and you reap what you sow. What are you willing to sow? Will you be a giver?

Understanding these common responses to money allows you to make better and smarter decisions that will help you to reap what you sow. Challenge yourself to move from a typical teenage response toward being able to invest in yourself so that you can ultimately become the giver you can be. Of course, the first step is being able to answer the question: Where is my money? Especially, if it's not in your account.

Excuses, excuses, excuses

"If you buy things you do not need, soon you will have to sell things you need."

– Warren Buffet

Have you heard the phrase, "The dog ate my homework?" I have heard this often from kids trying to explain how their homework just disappeared. It's the dog's fault; he ate it and it has nothing to do with forgetting or choosing not to do it. What about calling in "sick" when you have a deadline that somehow you were unable to get done because there just wasn't enough time? There are so many "reasons" that explain why you didn't do what you were supposed to do. Are these reasons or excuses? I'm guessing that you may be able to think about one or two other "reasons" why you were not able to do what you were supposed to do, especially when it comes to managing your money.

It's easy to make excuses for the lack of discipline required to take control of your money rather than taking responsibility for the fact that you just don't want to do it (for whatever "reason" you choose to believe). Maybe there is a reason, such as you don't know where to start. That's truly a reason, so invest in yourself and get some help. Figure out where to start. Congratulations on taking the first step by reading this book. You invested in yourself so that you can change your future.

Too often we rationalize excuses over why we chose not to do what we ought to do. What excuses have you allowed yourself to tolerate when it comes to your money and finances for running your business? What excuses are you allowing to prevent you from figuring out where your money is? You know it's not in your account, but what excuses prevent you from figuring out exactly where you spent your money? It's only when you know where your money is spent that you can take control of it.

Often, I hear the word "but" in the responses to the question, "Why don't you know where your money is?" After all, *money doesn't spend itself.* To be totally honest, I have to admit that there have been times in my life when I have used a "but" or two to explain why I became a little less focused and even a little lazy due to one excuse or another. Life is hectic and chaotic. And I know that trying to balance your personal and business life can be completely exhausting.

I also know that letting yourself "off the hook" with a "but" excuse will not create a long-term profitable outcome. It's impossible to run a long-term profitable business without a solid understanding of where you spend your money and how your money flows in and out of your account. Yet, it is often easier to say, "But you just don't understand," than to take responsibility for not managing your money.

Several common "but" excuses and responses that I've heard:

- *But you don't understand.*
- *But I am too busy.*
- *But there is not enough time.*
- *But if you only knew what I had to deal with.*
- *But it's too hard to balance work and my personal life.*
- *But you just don't get it.*

The "but" list is endless. I am sure that you can add a few more "but you…" statements that you have either heard or used once or twice. As difficult as this may be, the bottom line is that they are just excuses.

When you accept these statements as the excuses they are, you'll know exactly where your money is because you are able to make informed decisions about how to invest it as well as spend it. Let's delve deeper into the common excuses to discover how to address them.

Let's Delve Into Some of the "But" Excuses

But you don't understand.

Well, maybe I do; maybe I don't understand your specific situation. However, I **do** understand a few fundamental basics related to money. I understand that the same principles hold true whether we are talking about your personal or business finances. If you want to be able to sustain your lifestyle and your business, you need **cash**. Not only do you need it, you need to understand how it flows in and out of your personal and business accounts.

If you are unwilling to figure out where you spend your money and how to best manage it, know that:

- You will always be stressed about finances.
- It will be impossible for your business to thrive and grow.
- Without cash, your business will not survive.

Most likely I may not understand your specific situation or what you are dealing with in addition to money management. But I do understand one thing: money doesn't spend itself. Whether or not I understand is not as important as your understanding where your money is going so you can keep it in your account and pay your bills with less stress.

But I am too busy...(There is not enough time.)

If you asked a mother of triplets if she has ever been busy, I suspect the answer would be a resounding "yes." If you asked a millionaire if he or she has ever been busy, the answer would be a resounding "yes." If you asked your neighbor who has a child and an elderly parent if she is busy, the answer would be a resounding "yes!" If you asked the clerk at the checkout line if he has been busy, the answer would be "yes." If you asked yourself if you are busy, the answer would be "yes."

Life translates to ***busy*** every day. Our world of technology, which was supposed to streamline and simplify our lives, has actually made our lives even busier. Now everything is at our fingertips with mobile devices and we are supposed to get more done in less time.

Let me ask you to be honest with yourself. With all this technology at our fingertips, what are you really "busy" doing?

- Are you busy doing the right things to grow your business and create the life you want for your family?
- Are you a busy focusing on things that are not in line with your desires or priorities for your family and business?
- Are you so busy you have no idea what your real priorities are?
- Are you so busy with all these things that you have become a busy bee who flies between this and that and never really accomplishes anything?

The reality is that we all have 24 hours in a day to do what needs to be done. Do you use those 24 hours to align your priorities that will lead to growth in your business? Whether you want to admit it or not, figuring out and understanding how your money flows in and out of your account is vital to that growth and sustainability.

Why is it that some people can accomplish so much more than others in the same 24-hour period? Everyone is busy. After all, that's life.

Let's get real here.

- What do you accomplish in 24 hours?
- Are you taking care of your priorities or are you too "busy" with busy work?
- Are you making smart money decisions or are you too busy to bother?
- Are you setting up systems to know where your money goes or are you too busy to deal with it?

The truth is that if you are always too busy, you will be stressed and frustrated. You may even experience health issues as a result of the stress, lack of sleep, and frustration associated with being too busy. Yet we all have 24 hours.

Do you find yourself shuttling the kids from one practice to another? Dropping off one kid here, running to the grocery store, running home to put the groceries away, stopping back at the office, picking up your kid, and heading across town to pick up your spouse?

Do you find yourself picking up your phone and opening Facebook for just a minute; then start reading emails, just for a minute; then start scrolling through Instagram, just for a minute. Next thing you know, three hours have passed.

So, what can you do when you find yourself being too busy? What if you would commit to a proactive approach to time rather than a reactive one? If you want your business to sustain then you will have to find a way to allocate time to manage your money along with everything else; you have to.

You are going to be busy if you have any hope of taking care of your responsibilities. When you get home, you are going to be exhausted. And if you are unable to find a way to manage your time, you are going to struggle even more finding a way to manage your money. You are going to be so busy running around that there will not be time, at least when your eyes are open, to manage your finances in either your personal or business life.

By the time you get home, exhaustion takes over and you are asleep within 10 minutes of sitting down. Even if you start working on your finances, you find your head ends up on your keyboard and you are sound asleep.

So what can you do? Instead of focusing on what is the most pressing by reacting, start to take a proactive approach. One way to do this is to schedule your time in advance. It's called Time Blocking. What that means is you simply plan your week before your week starts. To begin, it will be challenging, but once it becomes a habit, I assure you, you will find it very useful. Grab your calendar and start by looking at the next week. You will most likely have commitments in place. So, we will work around those in this case.

See where you have an hour or couple of hours that you can "block" or schedule. You may find using a highlighter helpful, especially if you use a paper calendar. This works the same with an online version; just color code the section. Now, determine what you can schedule into that block of time.

- Maybe the kids have practice, so figure out a streamlined approach ahead of time how to manage practice drop off and pick up as well as maybe a grocery run on the way home. You have a few extra hands to help if it's on your way home.
- Maybe you can schedule client calls during a particular hour or block of time each day.
- Maybe you can schedule all errands on one day of the week.

Take this proactive approach and make sure you set aside time each week to work on your business. Schedule it in and stick to your schedule. Now you will have time scheduled to manage your money.

If you are willing to make this change and stick to it, you'll definitely find yourself less stressed and frustrated. Yes, busy is normal. For the most part, I do understand. What I understand is that:

- You must find a way to prioritize your responsibilities if you have any hope of accomplishing what needs to be done.
- You will have to get help if you want to get it all done.
- You have chosen to be an entrepreneur so that you can have a flexible schedule. That means that you create your schedule. If you don't like it, change it.

When you allow your life to become so busy, you will be stressed. Not only will you be stressed personally, but that stress will mirror and explode into your business life as well. As a business owner you have to juggle both personal and business responsibilities.

Often, all these tasks are overwhelming and there will be times where you'll have no idea what to do first, let alone second, third, and fourth.

There will be times when survival becomes your only focus and the only thing you are going to finish is the hottest and most pressing task in front of you.

There will be times when you are so busy trying to figure out how to manage family issues, kids, aging parents, spouses, friends, cooking, grocery shopping, and other commitments, as well as managing your business, that you will become so stressed your health will be affected.

Many times, there are so many priorities competing for your attention that it's extremely difficult to work in your business. By the time you sit down to work on your business, you are so exhausted you want to give up.

As you can see, if you are so busy that you cannot focus on your priorities, you will never figure out where your money is going so that you can make better decisions. You will continually be stressed when the bills are due because the money is not in your account.

Without taking time to manage your money, it will be impossible to create, let alone review, financial reports necessary for financial success. There is no way to figure out what areas need improvement; what areas are working and should be repeated. And there is absolutely no way to work smarter, only harder, because you are too busy.

Without the financials, it's almost impossible to create a budget or plan for the future, to estimate what money is needed for those unexpected or inevitable expenses. You are too busy.

The good news is you have 24 hours to work with. You can decide to make time to manage money. It's up to you. Money doesn't just jump out of your hands into someone else's unless you are too busy to pay attention to understand where it is going.

It's a challenge, this entrepreneurial way of life. You have to figure out how to be the manager, the marketing director, the employee, the boss, the bookkeeper, the goal setter, and the visionary, just for starters.

Don't let busyness be the reason you are too exhausted to figure out how to manage your money. That exhaustion will only lead to health issues, family issues, and eventually, business failure. Don't let yourself become so busy with tasks that do not align with your priorities, preventing you from living the lifestyle you desire.

The bottom line is when you are too busy to work on your business, to know your numbers, and to know how money flows in and out of your business, you will not be able to sustain a profitable and successful business. If you are too busy to run your business, then maybe you should opt for a job rather than running your own business. After all, you are too busy.

But you have no idea what I have to deal with.

You are right, I have no idea what you deal with specifically. But I do know that we still have the same 24 hours to work with. You may have to figure out how to deal with two-year-old toddlers and 90-year-old toddlers at the same time. You may have to deal with homeschooling your children due to a pandemic. You may have to deal with the loss of a job, a furlough, or closure of your business. You may have to completely change the way you do things. You may have to invest in technology just to survive. Your world may have been turned upside down. Your health may be failing. Your family may be facing the death of a loved one.

The truth is, I have no idea what you are facing or what challenges you are working to overcome.

The only thing that I **do** understand is that everyone must deal with challenges. Every successful entrepreneur faces challenges personally and professionally daily. Often these challenges are completely out of your control. In fact, if asked, most successful business owners would admit that they have to deal with a LOT of challenges, usually at the same time.

What is the difference between successful and unsuccessful entrepreneurs and small business owners? Successful ones choose:

- To make smart decisions during their 24 hours each day. They make decisions that are in alignment with their priorities and goals.
- To know and manage their money so that it will support those decisions.

What I found interesting while talking with folks was that more often than not, no matter what challenges I was facing, successful business owners had faced similar or worse situations over their entrepreneurial journey.

In a nutshell, it's up to you to decide whether challenges become an excuse or opportunity. Will you let the challenges distract you from doing what you need to do? Or will you let them become an opportunity to improve. You may not always be able to control the obstacles placed in your path, but you can decide to respond to those obstacles in a manner that aligns with your priorities, which will ultimately help you overcome those obstacles.

But it's hard to balance everything.

Balance… is there such a thing? In my opinion, no. You will never be able to maintain a 50/50 split between personal and business life. However, you must split your time and energy between both your personal and business life to be successful. In fact, your success is determined by how well you are able to achieve this so-called balance.

You know by now that you have 24 hours to work with. You also know that money management is crucial for success and must be included as part of your normal routine.

If you have been following the suggestions, you know that in order to even start to feel like you have balance in your life, you must find a way to manage your time so that you can manage your money. And the best part of the entrepreneurial journey is that if you don't like your schedule, you can change it.

In addition, there is something else that I understand about balance. You don't have to do it all by yourself. Support is not only available, it is necessary. If you think you can do everything on your own, you are mistaken. Of course, if you don't care if you succeed or fail, then feel free to do it all by yourself.

Whether you have to trade or barter some tasks, or whether you "convince" your kids or neighborhood kids to help take care of a few tasks, it's crucial to invest in support. There is a cost to this support. And that is something that you must consider. Start small. Choose a task that costs you more for your time than it would to have someone else just complete it for you.

Consider this: If you get support for a task that you no longer have to do, you can focus on more income-producing activities to support your business. Of course, step one is you must understand your finances. You must know what money is available to invest for this support. And it all starts by managing your money.

But you just don't get it.

Have you ever assumed that someone else just doesn't get it? I have, and there are definitely things that I don't get. But what I **do** get is that if you want to be a successful entrepreneur, you have to figure out how to make it work. And money management is a substantial part of the foundation of success.

If successful entrepreneurs have figured out how to do it, why can't you?

You can choose to figure out how work through health issues, situations with your kids, and caring for elderly parents along with a host of other challenges. And if you manage your money, money can give you more choices to solve those challenges.

I get that everyone has challenges to face, some of which are harder than others. The good news is that you are **only** responsible to face and overcome your challenges. You are responsible for you.

I get that if you want to own a successful and profitable business, you will become a good juggler. You will figure out how manage all the roles associated with your business. You will juggle serving as:

- the visionary who sets goals for the future and determines how to achieve them.
- the worker who has to get client work done.
- the manager who handles the challenges and coordinates tasks.
- the boss who makes sure the job gets done and provides support.
- the marketing director who establishes a recognizable brand.
- the bookkeeper who makes sure income and expenses are tracked.
- the accountant who keeps up with tax laws.

Yes, there are many roles that you must juggle. And juggling can be very exhausting. But what I get, that you must also get, is that when you own your own business, you have to figure out how to juggle all these roles. Yet, you don't have to be the one juggling them all by yourself. You will have to delegate some of the roles or at least some of the tasks to others. And you have to know what money is available to invest in these roles. And that starts by managing your money. It's up to you; money doesn't spend itself. And let's face it, figuring it all out is tough.

I don't get it all, but I do get a few things. And admittedly, over the years there were times that I have uttered one or more of these "but…" excuses. I allowed the "but" to be an excuse rather than opportunity for improvement. I made poor decisions because I believed that I was too busy and dealing with too much to focus where I knew I needed to.

And my health suffered. My priorities were out of alignment with my goals. I experienced shingles twice before age 40. Shingles is a disease that most medical experts say you will only experience once and is uncommon in those under 50. What's really interesting about shingles is that even though stress doesn't technically cause shingles, it does cause your immune system to weaken. And a weakened immune system puts you at risk for shingles.

Fortunately, a solid foundation provides the tools to overcome the "but" excuses more effectively when they arise. You know and understand you have a choice. You have a system in place that will make it possible to get back on track.

Are you willing to let excuses run your business? Or are you ready and willing to position your business for strategic profits? The choice is yours; money doesn't spend itself.

And You Wonder Why

"Clarity and simplicity are the antidotes to complexity and uncertainty."

~ General George Casey

Even when you know the importance of money management, there are times when you still wonder why your money seems to vanish before your eyes. I don't know about you, but I do have a suspicion why my neighbor may feel that way. I was looking out my window the other day and I noticed that my neighbor had received a delivery. There were several boxes, about 20 of them, on the front porch. Usually this is a daily occurrence. The tractor trailer pulls up to the garage and drops off the boxes.

Now, if we are being honest, I know that some of you know exactly what I am talking about. In fact, I may have just described your neighbor as well.

Truth be told, some of you are just as guilty. And I don't blame you. I often prefer to shop online instead of dealing with long lines. But let me ask you:

- When you open your cabinet, do you really need the eight bottles of the 64-oz. ketchup that was on sale? You may like ketchup, but eight?
- When you look at your shelves, are they overstocked?
- How often do you stop and grab a coffee or a mocha latte at your nearby coffee shop? Once, twice a week? Once a day?
- How often do you find it easier to eat out at your favorite restaurant than getting groceries and cooking at home? Two or three times a week?

- How often to you order online without thinking that you just placed an order yesterday?
- How often do you go on a shopping spree because you feel stressed and you find shopping is a great way to relax or reward yourself?
- How often do spend twice as much in gas for multiple trips back and forth from one event to another because you neglected to plan ahead?

If you don't believe that these little things add up, consider the following:

Let's say, you stop three days a week for coffee, three days a week for lunch, and two days a week for dinner. For argument's sake, let's assume the following. Yes, I know you don't like math, but bear with me. I will make this simple.

- Average Latte – $3.50. If you stop three days a week, the cost is a little over $10 a week.
- Average economical lunch – $10. If you stop three days a week, the cost is $30 a week.
- Average dinner – $20. If you stop two days a week, the cost is $40 a week.
- If you add just these three items together, as you have to eat and it's only a few dollars a few days a week, you'll realize that you are spending about $80 dollars a week, or roughly $320 dollars a month, and almost $4000 a year.

Do little charges add up? Yes! And yet you wonder why it seems as though your money vanishes from your account without a trace, yet money doesn't spend itself.

A Time to Reflect

Question #1: Where is your money?

1. When it comes to paying your bills, do you have enough money in your account every month to cover them?

   ❒ Yes

   ❒ No

2. Do you have a tracking system for your income and expenses?

   ❒ Yes

   ❒ No

3. Do you know each month whether or not you had more expenses or income?

   ❒ Yes

   ❒ No

4. Do you have money set aside to invest in assets for your business? (Equipment, software, support, professional development, and education)

   ❒ Yes

   ❒ No

5. Do you have the ability to run financial reports quickly so that you can "see" how your money flows?

   ❒ Yes

   ❒ No

~if you answered "Yes" to the above, keep up the great work.

~if you answered "No" to several of these questions, schedule a complimentary consultation at www.JanetIckes.com/ChatWithJanet to learn ways to turn those No's into Yeses.

INSPIRATIONAL THOUGHT:

TRUST IN THE LORD WITH ALL YOU HEART; AND LEAN NOT TO YOUR OWN UNDERSTANDING. IN ALL YOUR WAYS ACKNOWLEDGE HIM AND HE WILL DIRECT YOUR PATHS. PROVERBS 3:5–6 (ESV)

Reflection Journal

✓ Identify three items that you spend a little money on frequently. Example – coffee, lunch, etc.

- *1a* ______________________
- *2a*______________________
- *3a*______________________

What is the average cost of each item identified above?

★ *1b*____________________

★ *2b*____________________

★ *3b*____________________

How many times a week do you spend on each of the items above?

★ *1c*__________________

★ *2c*__________________

★ *3c*__________________

Now let's do the math:

★ *From the items above, enter the item, cost, and number of times a week you purchase each item in the respective boxes below. Now multiply (*) that cost by the cost per week by the number of times. What is the total for each item?*

- *1a*______: *1b*______ **1c*______ =____________
- *2a*______: *2b*______ **2c*______ =____________
- *3a*______: *3b*______ **3c*______ =____________

Example: if you spend $4.00 for coffee, three times per week, the math would be:

Coffee: $4.00 * (multiplied by) 3 = (equals) 12.

Now that you calculated it by week, multiply it by four to get an average per month. In the example above, that would equal almost $50. ($12 multiplied by 4 equals $48)

Add all three together. What do you get? ____________ (reminder this is a weekly amount and there are approximately four weeks in a month, and there arc 12 months in a year). Don't worry, I am not going to ask you to do any more math at this point.

Reflection Summary

of "Yes" answers from questions 1-5: ____________

~If you answered more "Yes" than "No" for questions 1-5, you are beginning to build your money foundation on rock. Keep up the good work.

What was the total of the three identified expenses per week? ____

~If this number surprised you, do something about it, especially if you struggle to pay your bills.

What is the total of just the three identified expenses per month? ____________________________________

~Ok, now it is time for math. Multiply the number above by 4. This is your monthly amount for just those three expenses. If this number is a little concerning, remember the choice is yours. Money doesn't spend itself.

What excuses have you made to avoid learning where your money is going? ___________________________

~Now that you identified it, do something about it.

What are you willing to change going forward? ______

~Set up a plan to change and move forward toward your goal.

Remember, it's up to you. Money doesn't spend itself.

Notes/Thoughts

Chapter 3

What Happens When "It All Breaks Loose?" And It Will...

"Expect the best. Prepare for the worst. Capitalize on what comes."

~ Zig Ziglar

It's morning! The alarm goes off and you reach over and hit the snooze button. Ahh…the alarm stops. Just a few more minutes… Of course, if you wouldn't have watched the game until 2 a.m., you may be a little more willing to open your eyes. The alarm blares again. This time you realize it's a half hour past the time you were supposed to get up – funny thing, you don't remember hitting that snooze multiple times.

Oh well, time to get up. Time to shower and put the contacts in. Wait… Where did that contact go? It dropped; it's here somewhere... gotta find it. There it is!

Now, coffee time. There are a few minutes to grab a cup before you have to leave. Wait… The timer didn't work. (May have had something to do with the fact that you were distracted before the game because you were scrolling through Facebook and failed to remember to set the timer).

Oh well. There is always the option to pick up a coffee from drive-thru on the way into the office before your first meeting. On the way in, you get behind "grandma" whose top speed is 25 in a 45-mph zone. You get held up at 16 stop lights and get cut off trying to turn into the parking lot. Finally, you make it to the office, and you realize that you left your phone at home along with your office keys.

Sound familiar? What are you going to do?

Are you going to throw your hands up and act like a two-year-old who didn't get the toy he wanted?

Are you going to get back in your car, go home and go back to bed? (It works for an ostrich. If danger is present, the ostrich will just bury their head in the sand).

Or are you going to ask to borrow a phone if needed and just make the best of the situation?

And maybe you can even count your blessings since your kids can't reach you for something unimportant.

Even better, you can view this as a teaching exercise for your kids to improve their initiative because they'll have to look up the office number to reach you if it is something important.

Question 2:
What happens when it all breaks loose?

"The key is this: meet today's problems with today's strength. Don't start tackling tomorrow's problems until tomorrow. You do not have tomorrow's strength yet. You simply have enough for today. "

~ Max Lucado

Are you prepared and willing to adjust and adapt to what life challenges you face, or would you prefer to stick your head in the sand like the ostrich? The ostrich simply sticks its head in the sand when it senses trouble. Even though the ostrich is about seven feet tall and can run up to 43 mph. Yet, when it becomes frightened, it chooses to stick its head in the sand in the hopes that trouble will just pass by. Do you bury your head in the sand like the ostrich especially when it comes to money matters?

Or do you choose to tackle to the situation at hand and adjust as needed to face your typical day? Will you bury your head or face the challenges head on?

What are you prepared for when life throws its curve balls?

Do you have a savings account or emergency fund to help defer financial stress when a paycheck doesn't arrive as expected or that sale falls through?

Have you ever noticed when you make great strides forward, everything seems to break loose? Suddenly, one challenge becomes several challenges no matter which way you turn. And it seems that challenges outnumber any strides forward. What are you going to do? Do you have a plan when your first plan, plan A, doesn't work? This second plan is considered a contingency plan or "plan B." A good example of plan B would be an emergency fund. This fund consists of money set aside for an emergency. What happens when a pandemic hits the country and your first two plans, A and B, aren't enough? Do you have a third plan, or plan C? This could be a savings plan that would cover three to six months of expenses. What about additional plans? Such as D, E, and F? Things happen. Life happens and you must be willing to adapt accordingly. Whether or not you have the additional plans in mind, you have to be willing to create them if necessary.

Just a typical day

"This is the day which the LORD hath made;
we will rejoice and be glad in it."

~ Psalm 118:24 (ESV)

What does your typical day consist of? More than likely, your typical day is filled with chaos and challenges. This type of day is the norm. But the bigger question is what you are going to do when you have to run your business during this typical day. What are you going to do when the plans you had in place have to change, while you adapt to meet the current needs of the typical day? Are you prepared with solid money management skills to provide a foundation that will sustain you while you face your typical day?

Considering that finances are mirrored in both your personal and business life, how you handle your typical day will be reflected in how you handle your typical day in business.

Does that mean that:

- You choose to believe that you are too busy to figure out where your money is going?
- In spite of the challenges in your typical day, you are determined to set aside time to make sure you know where your money is going?
- You proactively make decisions about your money before you spend it so that you can set up an emergency plan, plan B, and maybe even a savings account, plan C?

The bottom line is that not only do you have to figure out where your money is going, which is plan A, you also have to at least figure out plan B and C as well. In some cases, you may have to even come up with additional plans, D, E, and possibly (if things are really crazy), plans F and G just to survive. You can't prepare for all things that could go wrong, but having at least an emergency fund and savings account, plans B and C, would be a good start. Other plans can be developed as needed depending on your current situation.

When you are at least somewhat prepared for the curve balls that life throws at you, you can defer some of the financial stress when a paycheck doesn't arrive as expected or that sale falls through. These contingency plans sustain your business and lifestyle while you make the necessary adjustments.

Too often as you are moving toward accomplishing your project by the due date, something distracts and even prevents you from taking the next step forward. You never know when disaster may strike: your child may be involved in an accident; your elderly father may forget where he lives and head out to his home where he lived 70 years ago; your car may break down; your dog may become ill; or, a pandemic may occur halting many business functions and affecting life as it was.

What do you do? Give up on your deadline? Push back the due date? Or find a way to work through and meet your deadline the best you can? The choice is yours. You can give up or you can pivot and adjust, knowing you have at least plan B and C in place and are willing to create C, D, and E if necessary. Plan B, C, D and E…

"Someone's sitting in the shade today because someone planted a tree a long time ago."

~Warren Buffet

According to the parable of the sower, when the farmer threw out the seeds, some fell on rocky places, some on shallow soil, some in thorns, and some good soil. The seeds that fell on the rocky places withered and died. The seeds in shallow soil started to grow, but quickly died. The seeds in good soil were able to take root and grow. Those rooted in good soil were able to withstand the weather and grow and bear fruit.

Of course, fruit was the desired outcome. Just as in business, you have to root your seeds in good soil, and build a solid foundation if you intend to be profitable, or in this case, bear fruit.

In order to have a successful business that will support your lifestyle, you will have to make sure the seeds of your business land in good soil. That way the seeds can grow, and you will build a solid foundation. Knowing exactly how money flows in and out of your business is ingrained in those seeds necessary to build a solid foundation.

If you want your seeds to withstand the weather or challenges, and take root, grow, and bear fruit, you will have to incorporate at least plan B and C in order to keep the financial stress to a minimum during the challenging time. It's because you have plan B and C that your foundation can withstand the storms of life and remain financially stable.

What are you going to reap based upon what you sow now? Will you reap a financially stable lifestyle and business because you were willing to sow good seeds that fell in good soil and were able to grow and bear fruit? If you have a continency plan in place, you will build the foundation that can withstand the storms. And if you are willing to come up with a couple more contingency plans when the first six didn't work, you can even withstand a pandemic, instead of just your typical day.

When the challenges arise, you have a choice. You can "throw in the towel," or use the towel to mop up the sweat and step forward in spite of the challenges. When you have multiple plans, you can choose wisely how are you going to respond to your typical day.

We have started to build plan A. But when you have contingency plans, such as B and C, you will be less stressed dealing with these challenges that occur on a typical day or even the challenges that crop up completely unexpected.

What is an emergency fund? An emergency fund is simply an account outside of your normal operating account that acts as a safety net. It's a sum of money that is accessible to you in the event of a financial mishap or emergency.

Let's clarify what is considered an emergency. Better yet, let's clarify what is NOT considered an emergency. An emergency is not the urge to buy the newest and best product – something you just want for the sake of having it. However:

- if you need brakes on your car so that you can get back and forth to work.
- if you need to replace the hot water tank so that you can take a shower.
- if you need to replace a computer because it's how you earn your money and without it, your business would not exist.

Then you may consider using the emergency fund to cover these expenses. Keep in mind, that you must also have a plan in place to ensure that you replenish your emergency fund. You never know when:

- a serious health condition (such as a broken arm that requires an unexpected trip to the emergency room) or other health condition requiring hospitalization could come up.

- a piece of necessary equipment will break or simply wear out.

Here are some simple ways to get started so that you can save a little here and there for these kinds of emergencies:

- Make your morning coffee at home. If you make a cup of coffee at home every morning, take the money you normally would have spent on your morning run through the drive-thru and put it in a savings account. You will be amazed how quickly those few dollars add up.
- Save your change. Consider paying with cash and saving all your change. When you come home at the end of the day, put your change in a jar. When the jar is full, take it to the bank and put it into your savings account. All that change adds up quicker than you expect. My husband and I saved our change and were able to pay a minimum of two extra mortgage payments each year, which eliminated over seven years of a mortgage payment on our first home.
- Convert your credit card bonus points or rewards points into cash. Many credit cards and debit cards now offer rewards points for their everyday use. If you are disciplined with your credit cards and don't use them in place of cash, you can redeem for cash back and put them directly into your savings account. If you are not disciplined, choose a debit card for convenience until you build up your discipline for a credit card.

Now that you have plan B in place, what about plan C, a savings account? Start with a goal to set aside a financial reserve in an account separate from your operating account with a balance equivalent to three months of expenses. Yes, in order to know what amount to set aside, you must figure out what three months of expenses consist of. Nonetheless, this three-month reserve makes it possible to avoid stress when trouble happens, such as delayed payments or decreased sales during the summer or winter months, which can financially strain your business. You set aside money during the better times to assist in times that are not so good. That way your stress is reduced, even though times are tough.

When you achieve a balance of three months' expenses in the reserve account, increase to six months. Strive to prepare for a financial reserve of six months. How many businesses would be able to withstand a pandemic if they only had six months of expenses in reserve? Look at what is going on in today's economy. We are in unprecedented times. This pandemic crisis has created a completely new normal. We have been quarantined for months. Many are not able to work. And we certainly cannot connect like we once did. Networking in person is non-existent. Networking is now virtual using computers, streaming from individual homes.

In order to survive, you must pivot your processes and services so that they work in a virtual world. You have to figure out how to adjust for loss of income. You must account for your kids competing for your computer and the Zoom account. They have school and you have work. They need to be in class, and you have a team meeting.

You must juggle personal and business responsibility and finances to a new level. For the past several months, non-essential businesses have been shut down. Restaurants could only offer carry-out or delivery. Your outing consisted of a quick run to the grocery store. And worst of all, you cannot find toilet paper. Who would have thought a virus would cause toilet paper to be a scarce commodity?

You are instructed to remain in quarantine and stay home to reduce the spread of this virus. You are encouraged to practice "social distancing" and remain six feet apart at all times. Masks are to be worn when out and about. All because of this pandemic.

You are not able to work, and if you are, it's a completely different approach. Life has changed… If you want to survive, you have to figure out how to participate in virtual meetings, not live ones. You must figure out how you can offer your services virtually. Your survival depends on figuring it out. Businesses are closing. Life is completely different and a new normal is here. Are you prepared to withstand a pandemic?

Let's face reality: Surviving a pandemic may require more that plans B and C. So, what is your plan D and E? If you had a financial reserve in place to sustain your family for 30, 60, or 90 days, would that make a difference in your stress levels? What about six months or more? Have you even thought about it?

What could you focus on if you didn't have to focus on how you were going to pay your bills for the next 30, 60, or 90 days? Without the survival mentality, would you be able to focus your time and energy towards pivoting your business towards income-producing activities that meet the standards of the new normal? What difference would it make if you had B and C in place before the pandemic hit?

Ask yourself: What are you willing to **not** spend on today so that you can spend on what's necessary tomorrow?

Life is full of "unexpected" turns that pop up in front of us. After all, it's just a typical day. And you never know what is going to happen on a typical day, like if your typical day will include facing a pandemic.

Meet the new neighbors.

"To expect the unexpected shows a thoroughly modern intellect."

~ Oscar Wilde

Have you ever heard the expression, "Expect the unexpected?" Life is full of unexpected surprises. These surprises can be good, bad, or devastating. But one thing for certain: life is full of twists and turns. In fact, it's when you are working through your typical day that the new neighbors seem to move in.

These new neighbors are known as Murphy and Mayhem. Have you ever noticed that when you are facing several challenges, that's when additional challenges arise? You've heard of Murphy's Law: "Anything that can go wrong, will go wrong." What about Mayhem, otherwise known as chaos? Hence, the neighbors, Murphy and Mayhem.

Typical days are filled with mayhem and chaos. It seems that when something goes wrong, everything seems to go wrong. If your car is down for maintenance, what are the "odds" that your spouse's car will also break down in the same week? What are the odds that when your hot water tank breaks, your fridge stops working, your oven does not turn on, and the air conditioner starts blowing hot air, all in the same week? It seems if it can go wrong, it does. Hence Murphy's Law. And in my world, where Murphy is present, Mayhem is not far behind.

It seems when you are finally making progress toward your goal, Murphy or Mayhem try to move in. Just when you finally pay off your car, the transmission needs replacing. Just when you get your credit card paid off, your spouse needs surgery and has to be off work for several months. Just when your business starts to bring in more revenue than ever before, a virus halts all future sales because your business is considered non-essential.

Sales as you knew it, gone. Revenue you expected, non-existent. And of course, that is exactly when the new neighbors, Murphy and Mayhem move in. It never seems to fail; when one crisis pops up, another one joins it.

I am sure you have experienced similar situations yourself, perhaps several times in your life. In my experience, when Murphy and Mayhem arrive, it's a package deal. They move in together. In fact, one comes in the front door, the other in the back door. They are great friends who enjoy your company and do everything possible to join you, wherever you are. They are good neighbors who move right in, especially when you least expect them. Of course, the pandemic has put a major light on the reality of expecting the unexpected. But even before the COVID-19 pandemic, Murphy and Mayhem have most likely moved in down the street, next door, or already occupy space in your spare room. Even if you've kicked them out once or twice, somehow, they both end up back in your house, watching TV with you in the living room.

If Murphy causes an emergency, do you have plan B in place? What happens when you need $1,000 to cover an emergency? Is it available? Or are you going to be in the two-thirds of Americans who will struggle to scrounge up $1,000 in an emergency?

Money Factoid: Two-thirds of Americans would struggle to scrounge up $1,000 in an emergency[8]*. ~The Associated Press-NORC Center for Public Affairs Research*

What choices do you have if you are unable to work, your business is forced to close, and life as you know it completely turns upside down? What happens when your health prevents you from working? What happens in the middle of chaos when more challenges arise? What happens when plans B, C, and D are just not enough?

What if a smaller expense arises? Do you have at least $400 in savings to cover the cost of a couple of tires for your car?

If you are like most Americans, the answer is "no." You will have to put the $400 charge on a credit card because you don't even have a little put away. Now your debt increases, unless you have a plan to pay for this unexpected expense.

Money Factoid: For most, $400 will cause most to use their credit card[9]*. Source: 2018 Survey of Household Economics and Decision- Making Report*

What is going to happen when you need four tires? Is that going to cause significant stress, frustration, and fear? Of course, walking or taking the bus are always options.

Do you have any plan in place to deal with Murphy and Mayhem? Considering most people don't even think of plan B, odds are plan C, D, and E are not even something acknowledged, until maybe now.

If you want to be successful, profitable, and reduce your stress when it comes to money, you must begin to set money aside for plans B and C. Start with the minimum plan B of a $1,000 emergency fund. Then work towards plan C with at least three months of reserve available. Both of these plans tend to be great repellents to both Murphy and Mayhem. Is it hard? Of course, but it can be simple.

Let's face it, life throws curve balls. Something often goes wrong. Something pops up unexpectedly that requires cash. It can be stressful or not. The choice is yours. Are willing to set up plan B and C? Are you willing to pivot as need be?

If you believe that you will never need Plan B, C or D, or you're confident that an emergency will not arise just when you least expect it, then by all means focus your attention elsewhere. However, if it is at all possible that at some point, you will meet these neighbors, Murphy and Mayhem, who will likely find a way to move into your house, I encourage you to figure out a way to set aside a few dollars now before it's too late. Sound impossible? It's not! Remember, money doesn't spend itself.

How would it feel to be like the one-third of Americans who had at least a $1,000 in emergency funds set back? How much stress could you eliminate if you could pay cash for an unexpected $400 expense, rather than put it on credit card that has to be paid later?

Whether it's in your personal or business life, are you prepared, at least a little?

How would you feel if you could pay to replace the transmission when your spouse is out of work because you had money set aside as plan B? What if you could still make the mortgage payment even when your "non-essential" business is closed for the next several months because you created a plan C? What if you could evict your guests, Murphy and Mayhem, who moved into your spare room? If you had even a little set aside to defer the stress from the chaos and challenges that are bound to arise, how would it feel?

When you have a system in place to fund your emergency account to cover those unexpected expenses, it goes a long way to repel both Murphy and Mayhem, as well as reducing your stress levels. Having savings set aside for when the unexpected happens or something critical needs to be replaced gives you the opportunity to breathe while you figure out where to go next.

Of course, you cannot "plan" for every specific ordeal that may create a financial strain or possibly affect your financial stability in a negative way. But you **can** keep the stress associated with the unexpected minimized when you have money set aside in plan B and C. The reality is that these expenses are not unexpected; they are inevitable. You just didn't know exactly when they would show up.

Keep in mind that for an emergency fund and savings account to be useful, both should be set up as separate accounts. Although you should be able to access them if needed, the access should not be so easy that you are tempted to use the funds whenever you feel that you want, just because you want something.

Be sure that when the true emergencies arise, the money is available in that account to reduce the stress associated with that unexpected, inevitable expense. Murphy and Mayhem can move out. And you will have the peace of mind to know that you can handle those expenses without completely crushing your financial stability.

Don't forget though, this is an ongoing process. Once the plans are in place, you must have a plan to replenish these funds as they are used. That way, Murphy and Mayhem can move out for good. You will still have your financial foundation in place, year after year. But it's your choice since money doesn't spend itself.

Respond, Don't React.

"The quickest way to double your money is to fold it in half and put it in your back pocket."

~ Will Rogers

Looking back in history, I am really surprised how history repeats itself. It makes me realize that we apparently didn't learn our lessons very well. During the US Housing Crisis in 2008, U.S. foreclosures spiked by more than 81%,[10] according to a CNNMoney report.

A total of 861,664 families lost their homes to foreclosure,[11] according to RealtyTrac. What's really sad is it could have been prevented in many cases. If the average family had six months of expenses in reserves, the crisis could have been prevented. How much do you have set aside right now?

If you are among the majority of Americans, odds are you don't have money set aside. According to Credit Donkey, approximately 28% of adults have no savings set aside and an estimated 38 million households in the U.S. live hand to mouth, meaning they spend every penny of their paychecks.[12]

Right now, we are in a pandemic, and some are not sure when the next paycheck will arrive. Yet, what a difference it would make if you had six months of expenses saved. Even three months or one month would have made a major difference because then you would have had a choice to respond rather than react.

Picture this: Your dog runs through the house in delight to greet you as you return home. Unfortunately, on the way across the living room to shower you with love simply because you are home, he bumps into the stand with your antique lamp. In slow motion, you watch your treasured lamp land on the floor, shattering into 1,000 pieces.

Do you react, immediately getting angry, yelling at your dog, and upsetting both you and your best friend? This is not going to put any of the 1,000 pieces back together. Or are you going to respond, realizing you are reacting in anger, choose to pause, and take a deep breath? Yes, you are devastated, but your dog was merely expressing his excitement and joy to see you.

Do you react or respond when:

- You get cut off on the highway?
- Another motorist takes the parking space that you were about to pull into?
- Your child tests the boundaries you set?

What are your first thoughts and actions? What is the result from your reaction or response? Is the result positive or negative?

Remember, your personal reaction or response will mirror in your business. Contemplate whether you will react or respond to the challenges you will have to face; to the chaos that is inevitable; to the difficulties you will have to deal with.

Equipment breaks, clients are challenging, your team may miss deadlines, or technology may fail. Are you going to react or respond? Will you react with emotion, increase your stress level, and potentially cause yourself a lot more issues because you reacted in anger? Or are you going to respond by taking a deep breath so that the emotion dissipates, and you can respond in a way that will allow you to move forward?

Reaction is emotional and instinctual, often based in anger and fear of the unknown. Reactions are fueled by the lack of preparedness. It's like a puppy that hasn't been trained. That untrained puppy is going to bark at the passing neighbor. He is going to help himself to your dinner as soon as you turn your back. In contrast, responding is being more thoughtful. You find ways to explore outcomes before you speak. You weigh the pros and cons and consider what is best for yourself and others in the situation. Responses are more like a well-trained dog that comes when called, barks to alert you to something he sees as potentially dangerous, and waits patiently for his treat after you have eaten your dinner.

What happens when you choose to respond rather than react? What happens when you choose to act like the well-trained dog rather than the untrained puppy? Will you be able to adapt and work through the chaos of your typical day? Will you be able to handle those unexpected expenses that you knew you were eventually going to have to deal with? Will you be able to withstand the storms of life because you chose to build your foundation on rock instead of sand?

It's impossible to know when your health will take a downward turn or when maintenance of critical appliances and equipment is necessary. That's why it is imperative that you start building your emergency fund and setting aside money for that "rainy day," as grandma used to say. Do this as soon as possible so that you can manage these emergencies by responding rather than reacting to the unexpected expenses that will inevitably arrive.

One of the ways I have found to help me respond rather than react is to recite the following:

"God, grant me the serenity to accept the things I cannot change, courage to change the things I can, and wisdom to know the difference."

~ Reinhold Niebuhr

It gives me the time to pause, to breathe. It gives me the space needed not to react.

Of course, when you have "one of those days" and everything seems to be going wrong, odds are emotions will take over and you will forget to pause, and definitely fail to recite anything to mitigate the emotions before additional complications arise.

Recently, I found myself in a position of the untrained puppy that reacted on impulse and emotion. I found myself letting anger serve as my decision maker. There was no deep breath, no pause, and no logic. Just anger and negative emotion. Some may have viewed the situation as a justifiable reaction, but the resulting decisions made in anger were not.

When anger drives your decisions, you often do not make smart ones. Instead you end up making choices that cause the situation to become worse. After an argument with my teenager, I attempted to keep my mind off the situation. So, I angerly took items out to put in the trunk of our car. Since my hands were full, I used my elbow to pop up the trunk lid, with way more force than needed. I soon realized a great, unforgettable lesson: what goes up must come down! I suggest that you do not try to use your forehead to stop the trunk lid when it recoils back down. It's likely to cause a concussion, making it extremely difficult to focus and stand any type of light source for the next several weeks. Clearly taking a deep breath so that I could respond rather than react would have been a much better choice.

Have you found yourself in similar situations? Were you so stressed that you made a quick decision that was not in your best interest? We are human and often react with emotions rather than responding with thought. But you do have a choice. You don't have to get a lump on the head before you choose to pause, take a step back, and evaluate the situation. You can make a better, smarter decision and respond to the challenges at hand.

And you don't have to get a lump on your head before you choose to take control of your money so that you can respond instead of react when life throws you a few curve balls. Respond to Murphy and Mayhem. Don't react. Respond with a plan B at the minimum and work towards plan C. Don't react with emotion. It's up to you. You have a choice because money doesn't spend itself.

Remember, it's up to you. Money doesn't spend itself.

A Time to Reflect

Question #2: What are you going to do when it all breaks loose?

1. Do you have at least a $1,000 emergency fund (plan B) set up?

   ❒ Yes

   ❒ No

2. Do you have a savings account with a three-month expense reserve (plan C) in place?

   ❒ Yes

   ❒ No

3. Do you respond instead of react to challenges you face?

   ❒ Yes

   ❒ No

4. Do you have funds set aside for future expenses, such as new equipment or software?

   ❒ Yes

   ❒ No

5. Do you have the option to use cash instead of a credit card for a $400 expense?

   ❒ Yes

   ❒ No

~if you answered "Yes" to all the above, you are well on your way to financial success.

~if you answered "No" to several of these questions, schedule a complimentary consultation at www.JanetIckes.com/ChatWithJanet to learn ways to turn those No's into Yeses.

Inspirational Thought:

I Can Do All Things Through Christ Who Strengthens Me ~ Philippians 4:13 (ESV)

Reflection Journal

✓ What amount do you have in your emergency fund? __________

- If you do not have at least $1000 in each, how much more do you need? ______________________
- If you are under $1000, what can you do to add money as quickly as possible? _______________

✓ What expenses are you planning for? List three and the estimated amount of each.

- _________________Amount_________________
- _________________Amount_________________
- _________________Amount_________________

Examples include equipment replacement, software, professional development.

✓ What amount do you have in a savings account to cover expenses? ____________________

- How many months of expenses will it cover? ____

Inspirational Thought:

But They Who Wait For The Lord Shall Renew Their Strength; They Shall Mount Up With Wings Like Eagles; They Shall Run And Not Be Weary; They Shall Walk And Not Faint. ~ Isaiah 40: 31 (ESV)

Reflection Summary

of "Yes" answers from questions 1-5: ____________

~If you answered more "Yes" than "No" for questions 1-5, you are on your way to figuring out what to do when it all breaks loose. Keep up the good work.

✓ *Do the math:*

What is the total of the three identified expenses? _____

(add them all together)

Now, set up an automatic transfer that totals the amount of the identified expenses. Transfer this amount to a separate account so that it's available when it's time to pay the bill.

What date did you schedule the transfer for? ________

Notes/Thoughts

Chapter 4

Now What? It Seems So Overwhelming.

"Believe you can and you are halfway there."

~ Theodore Roosevelt

It's not easy being an entrepreneur. It's not easy to manage money, either in your personal or business life. It's not easy, but it is simple. You can take one step at a time. The process is not as complicated as you may think. I have laid out step by step guidance and provided resources and tools to make the process simple, so that you can begin to build a solid money management system. This is a simple system that you can begin to use today. And the best part is that these tools are adaptable to both personal and business finances.

Now what? It's time to EXCEL!

EXCEL

***E**xpect the unexpected; it's really inevitable*

***X** out the excuses*

***C**hoose to commit to managing your money, one step at a time*

***E**xplore ways to streamline workflows and delegate tasks*

***L**ook over and review your numbers consistently*

To excel, you must take the steps to build a solid financial foundation. A foundation that is like the wise man, built on rock not sand. That way, you can sustain financial stability in spite of challenges in your business and personal life. You will set yourself up for success. You will have a business that has solid financial systems in place to support profits, growth, and your personal lifestyle.

"The secret to getting ahead is getting started."

~ Mark Twain

Are you ready to take the first step? Great! Let's get started.

Question 3: Where do I start?

"Take the first step in faith. You don't have to see the whole staircase, just take the first step."

~ Martin Luther King Jr.

I understand that for many people, numbers are overwhelming and money management is even more overwhelming. And when you are overwhelmed, you become confused. And a confused mind does nothing. So, I want to take out most of the overwhelm right now. The process is laid out in a simple step-by-step method that you can follow.

And if you are willing to follow the steps, you will find yourself able to reduce your stress when it comes to money because you will know where your money is being spent and how it flows through your account. You will be able to make better decisions because you have good plans in place to deal with the unexpected, inevitable occurrences in life. You will be able pay yourself because you have taken the time to understand and manage the money that flows in and out of your account proactively rather than reactively.

To guide you on this journey, don't forget to take advantage of my special bonus gift just for you.

Download the *Know Where Your Money Is Toolkit* today. Inside this toolkit is access to downloadable templates that you can customize to start tracking your income and expenses and creating a budget. In addition, you will find several checklists to help keep you focused and on task.

Just go to https://JanetIckes.com/MoneyToolKit and let me know where to send your bonus kit.

How do you start? You Eat an Elephant

"Spend more time on the solution than with the problem."

~ Tony Robbins

Have you ever heard how to eat an elephant? You eat an elephant, one bite at a time.

Bite 1: Separate your business and personal accounts

I am shocked that so many entrepreneurs and small business owners do not realize how important it is to separate their business and personal accounts. Since it is their own business, they did not even consider that their business funds and personal funds should be separate or that this is even necessary.

Why is it so important to separate your business and personal accounts? First and foremost, it is the only way to know exactly how your business is doing on its own. If you mix in personal money, and try to track your numbers, the blended numbers make it impossible to really know how profitable your business is. There is just no way to tell because the money is co-mingled.

Now, let's face facts. As an entrepreneur you may support your business with personal funds. This is quite common especially when you are starting out. Personal contributions are not a problem. The problem lies when you don't know how much money you personally contributed to the business.

Without knowing your financial contribution to your business, you may believe that your business is profitable. However, the truth may be that your own contributed money is the only reason that your business is profitable. And if you are putting so much of your own money into your business to make it profitable, the truth is, your business is not profitable at all.

Without separation of accounts, it makes it difficult to impossible to know just how profitable your business is.

Secondly, there are different tax implications when it comes to owner contributions (personal money you put into your business) and owner withdrawals (personal money you take out of your business). Therefore, you must track them accordingly. Keeping separate accounts provides a simple way to track these transactions.

One more thing to consider is that should your tax accountant deem it in your best interest to classify your business as a Limited Liability Corporation (LLC), the only way you can claim liability protection for your personal assets is if you do not co-mingle personal and business money.

There must be a very clear distinction of exactly what money is business-related with no comingling of personal money. And if you cannot prove which income and expenses are personal vs. business because you chose not to separate your business and personal accounts, you have just pierced that veil of protection.

So, take the first bite and separate your business and personal accounts. Now.

Bite 2: Track your Income and Expenses

"You can't manage it if you can't measure it."

~ Peter Drucker

"If you can't measure it, you probably can't manage it. Things you measure tend to improve."

~ Ed Seykota

You must find a way to track your numbers, especially your income and expenses. Tracking these numbers is essential to your success. The method does not have to be complicated. It can be simple. The bottom line is that you can't manage what you cannot measure. You can't measure what you don't track. In other words, you must write it down in some way, using a consistent method that allows you to show the numbers for both your income and expenses consistently.

Tracking is the only way to know if you are profitable. Profits mean that your income was higher than your expenses. Profits are vital to long-term sustainability. Profits from your business provide the paycheck to sustain your personal lifestyle.

Secondly, tracking allows you to determine whether or not you have met your financial goals. The goals provide direction. The only way you know what is working and what needs to be improved is whether or not you achieve those goals. Without tracking, you have no idea.

Without tracking you may make financial decisions that are not beneficial and supportive to your priorities.

Picture throwing darts at a dartboard. Your goal is to throw the dart so that it hits the center of the bullseye. That way you have achieved the desired goal. If the darts are your efforts, activities, and time that is spent on your business and the bullseye is your desired goal, it makes sense that you must throw the dart towards the bullseye if you want to be successful and profitable.

If you don't track your numbers, you may be throwing your darts at the bullseye in front of you, yet in reality, the dart board is behind you. Would you agree that it may be next to impossible to achieve the goal of a bullseye? Tracking allows you to know where the bullseye lay and allows you the ability to determine how to hit that bullseye consistently.

Ok, I can hear it now: "But that is too complicated." No, that is only an excuse. You have options. There are simple options and ways to begin to track your numbers and track your income and expenses so that you know you are aiming your darts at the bullseye.

One option, which has been available for many, many years, involves paper and a pen (or pencil if you prefer). Yes, this is an option. And it's one that works well for some. And if that is you, great. Grab a piece of paper and pen and write down all your income and expenses. You can model the Basic Income and Expense Tracker to get started.

Another option is one that involves using computer software. Computer software eliminates some of the repetitive, time-consuming tasks, such as adding and subtracting and allows you to use some of the functions and features of the software to automate such tasks.

Yet another option is to invest in a software specifically designed to not only automate those repetitive tasks but make it simple to research and report on how money is flowing in and out of your account. All records are available in one place, which allows additional workflow and processes to be automated and streamlined.

Of course, with each software there is a learning curve. And depending on your experience and abilities, which system works best for you is completely up to you.

You just must figure out which system is best for you. And it's a simple answer. What is the best system for you? **The one you are going to use!**

What is the best system for you? The one you are going to use!

Now let's explore some of the benefits and drawbacks of your options so that you can make a good decision. So, for starters, grab paper and pen and write down every penny that flowed in and out of your account for the past 30 days.

Don't make it complicated. Don't overthink it. Just do it.

If you like pen and paper, model your paper using the template below. If you prefer using a software program, such as MS Excel or Google sheets, feel free to download the Basic Income and Expense Tracker from your bonus *Know Where Your Money Is Going Toolkit* at https://JanetIckes.com/MoneyToolKit. Update and adapt this tracking spreadsheet to meet your needs.

Basic Monthly Income and Expense Tracker			Month:	
Income Tracker				
		(user to identify various income sources)		
Date	Total Amount	Income	Income	Income
1-Jun	100	100		
5-Jun	250		250	
8-Jun	300		300	
10-Jun	500			500
12-Jun	350	350		
Income Total	**1500**	**450**	**550**	**500**
Expense Tracker				
Date	Total Amount	Advertising	Rent	Utilities
2-Jun	250	250		
9-Jun	500		500	
14-Jun	50	50		
18-Jun	250			250
Expense Total	**1050**	**300**	**500**	**250**
Totals from above...				
Monthly Analysis				
Income Total	**1500**	*Income*		
Expense Total	**1050**	*Minus Expenses*		
Profit/Loss	**450**	*Equals Profit/Loss*	*If the number is greater than zero, then congratulations; you have a profit. If it's less than zero, you experienced a loss.*	

Using the template above is a simple way to start to build your foundation. However, it's imperative that you track **both** your income and expenses **consistently** month by month.

I mentioned two common options for spreadsheet software, Google sheets and Microsoft Excel. Both will allow you to automate adding and subtracting by taking advantage of the formula feature within the software. There are pros and cons to both. Google is a free software program, whereas depending on the version, MS Excel may involve an investment. I have used MS Excel for many years and find this software to have more capabilities than Google sheets.

Again, the best process is the one you will use. One of the main reasons to utilize a spreadsheet is to automate the addition and subtraction required to figure out your totals for each month. The Basic Income and Expense Tracker template includes the basic formulas needed to do just that. It's a starting point.

In addition, a spreadsheet allows you to make corrections to individual transactions quickly and automatically update your totals. In other words, it will "do the math for you." The formulas will automatically update your totals, making the whole process a little faster. But you must have at least a basic understanding of how the spreadsheet functions in order to use it effectively.

Depending on your situation, a better option may be to invest in a software program designed specifically to manage your money with automated and streamline processes already built in. Several options are available to choose from. I am only going to mention the one that I personally use, which is QuickBooks Online, as it is specifically designed for small business owners. There are others available, but my personal preference is one of the QuickBooks Online versions. Which one to choose depends on your specific situation. Speak to an expert first to determine the specifics for each level or version before making the final decision.

Feel free to check out the additional resources which will provide you with a little direction as to what spreadsheet and QuickBooks options are available. Check out the resources on www.JanetIckes.com/Resources.

Investing in a software program such as QuickBooks may be in your best interest. Remember, when you evaluate an expense for software, you must take into consideration that it is an investment in your business. Streamlining and automating the financial tracking is a tradeoff of your time. Is your time worth more than the investment in the software? Will the investment provide the result in a more efficient and effective manner? If the answer is "yes," then the investment may be very beneficial.

To get a bigger picture, let's take a look at a few key benefits to consider when evaluating a software program, such as QuickBooks, which is specifically designed to manage your money. At least you will know what to look for.

Benefit 1 – Automation

One of the easiest ways to improve efficiency is to automate basic tasks. Automation allows you to spend less time on necessary tasks so that you have more time to focus on income- producing ones. What are some tasks that make great first steps to automate?

1: Receipts

Often, business owners get overwhelmed when it comes to not only keeping but organizing receipts for tax purposes. These receipts get shoved into your pockets, under mounds of paperwork, under your car seat, and in the corner, and ultimately may end up in the trash, completely forgotten. If you are asked by the IRS to provide support for a specific expense, good luck finding it in the dumpster.

Cash items can also get out of control. If you pay cash and you fail to write it down, you have no what you spent or how often you spent it. I assure you, these unknown expenses can add up quickly.

Would it be helpful to take a picture of the receipt when you make the purchase? What if you had a mobile app that would let you scan the receipt on the spot? QuickBooks has this mobile functionality built into the mobile app for the software. You can use your phone to scan the receipt and a lot of the information will automatically upload into your software database. It also attaches a picture to the specific transaction as support. Now, all you need to do is file it in a yearly folder as backup. And if you need to find it, it's conveniently attached as a picture to the transaction, right at your fingertips.

2. Transaction Details

Depending on the number of transactions flowing in and out of your account, the sheer volume can be extremely time consuming. Yet, you know that tracking all your income and expenses is vital to your ultimate success.

So, writing it down manually may not be the best approach. Although, it does work and for some, it will work just fine. At some point, you must really look at how much time it takes to manually track this information. Then, evaluate the amount of time for the manual process against the time needed to meet your goal and the investment in a software that will streamline the process. Is your time worth manually taking care of something that is necessary but doesn't produce income?

Another advantage of the specifically designed software is that transactions can be automated. The automatic download reduces the amount of time required to manually write or key the information directly into a spreadsheet. This software connects directly to your bank account, reducing the need to manually type or key in information.

This automation significantly reduces the data entry, saving a lot of time and effort. The basic data is already in your software. The only thing left is to add a few specific details if needed and determine the type of transaction – income or expense. The coding allows you to group the same type of expenses together and automatically totals them.

This software also has built-in reports that use this information to provide financial information as well as tax information quickly. The exact information you need to make better decisions, determine if you are close to achieving your goals, and help you comply with tax requirements.

Benefit 2 – Organization

When you take advantage of a software program, all your information is kept in one spot or database. This database allows you to find transactions using keyword searches within the database. And let's face it, a computer can search and find specific info a lot faster than a human can by searching through mounds of paper files and folders.

Having this ability to locate information at your fingertips allows you to make better decisions because you have a better understanding of exactly what the transaction is that flowed in or out of your account.

Benefit 3: Reports

Another advantage of investing in technology is the reporting abilities. In fact, software designed for money management includes reports that are built in. In other words, the reports are designed so that you can quickly run them based upon the information in your database.

In fact, the key reports necessary to understand for your business are part of the package. This reporting capability makes it very simple to produce the reports that you need to look at, review, and analyze so that you can determine your profitability, your strengths, and your areas of improvement. Reviewing these key reports are vital to the profitable longevity of your business. And it's part of the foundation necessary for future growth.

What are the key reports you need to be able to produce on a regular basis? They are:

- Profit and Loss Statement
- Balance Sheet
- Cash Flow Statement

Let's keep it simple and take a look at an overview of each of these key reports. You only need to have a basic understanding so that you can make better decisions. As time goes on, you will understand, more in depth, the value and function of each report. For now, I just want you to grasp a basic understanding of the key reports and the general information provided for each report.

- *Profit and Loss Statement*-This report summarizes all your income and expenses for a particular period of time. Then the report subtracts your expenses from your income to show you if you were profitable. You are profitable if your income is higher than your expenses for that period of time. If your expenses are higher than your income, you have a loss for that period of time.
- *Balance Sheet*-This report shows the value of your business at a specific point in time. It summarizes your assets. Assets constitute what your business owns, such as cash, equipment, and vehicles. It also summarizes your liabilities. Liabilities are what you owe, such as loans and credit card balances. As the name suggests, somehow this report must balance or equal out in total. All that means is that there is a third part to this report, known as the equity in the business. In a nutshell, assets equal the addition of liability and equity, hence the name Balance Sheet. Basically, equity is the difference between the assets and liabilities. This report accumulates the value of your business, year after year, making it a great indicator as to the strength and sustainability of your business.
- *Cash Flow Statement*-This report focuses solely on how cash flows in and out of your business. Cash is the lifeblood of any business. What is on this report? Think about how cash is represented in your business. Cash flows in and out of your business in the form of income and expenses. Yes, you can find this on the Profit and Loss Statement. However, what about cash used for liabilities and the actual cash in the bank? That information

is found on the Balance Sheet. You see, when it comes to cash, you find some information on the Profit and Loss and some information on the Balance Sheet. The Cash Flow Statement blends the cash items from both reports.

These are the key financial reports that all small business owners must not only become familiar with but must review and understand. As the owner, you don't have to code the transactions that flow to these reports, but you must understand and review them regularly. Start with a basic understanding. As you review and work with these reports, you will understand more and more why they are essential to your business.

It astonished me how many small business owners and entrepreneurs never looked at these reports. Now that you know what they are, and the basic function of each, you can see how vital they are for building your solid financial foundation.

The only rationale for not looking at these reports is if you're experiencing so much profit, it doesn't matter. If that's the case, you have a choice to review them or not. The entrepreneurs who have so much money that it really doesn't matter not only look at their key financial reports, they actually study them.

Don't be like many entrepreneurs and small business owners who don't look at these reports or throw them in drawer and play "ostrich." Otherwise, you will wonder where your money has gone because it's not in your account and you'll have no idea what you are going to do when it all breaks loose.

Bite 3: Create a Budget; it's only a four-letter word

"Plan your work and work your plan."

~ Napoleon Hill

What is a budget? According to Dave Ramsey, a budget is telling your money where to go instead of wondering where it went. Unfortunately, most wonder where their money goes because they don't keep a budget. According to US Bank Possibility Index, only 41% of Americans keep a budget, which means almost 60% do not.[13]

If you want to tell your money where to go, then keep a budget. In my opinion, budget is just a four-letter word. For a budget is simply a PLAN. A budget lets you plan:

- The direction you want your business to go.
- How much money you need to achieve your goals both short term and long term.
- What expenses you have.
- What income is expected.
- For unexpected expenses that will inevitably arrive.

Then you compare your plan to the actual numbers so that you can steer the direction of your business, have the money available to achieve your goals, be prepared for upcoming expenses that are unexpected (or expected), and ultimately make better decisions.

Now you can focus your time, energy, and efforts, based upon numbers and facts, not on emotions.

Early on in our marriage, my husband and I had to come to an understanding about money. Anyone who lives with another person will eventually, at some point, have to come to an understanding about money. What is remarkable though is how often opposites attract, especially when it comes to money. And we are no different than most.

My husband likes to spend; I prefer to save. Together, it works, most of the time. The key is to come to an agreement about money. You may need to find a compromise, or middle ground, if you want to stay together for any length of time.

For us, we found a compromise that provided each of us a little money each month to use on whatever we wanted without consulting the other. We could spend this money solely at our discretion. Anything over this amount had to be discussed before the money was spent.

Being the numbers person in our relationship, I "ran the numbers" and came up with the monthly amount. My husband agreed. Of course, thinking back, it may have been largely because he preferred not to deal with numbers, and newlyweds tend to try to make one another happy.

Nonetheless, the compromise worked for several years. Then my husband had a brilliant revelation that was revealed to him when he started to listen to coworkers who convinced him that our plan wasn't fair, at least to him. Why? His job was very seasonal. Being a coal truck driver, his pay was based on the number of loads hauled during the pay period. Consequently, there were times of the year when he made significantly more money than in others, as these loads were affected by the weather. My job, on the other hand, was salaried and I received the same pay every two weeks regardless of the hours worked.

His allowance, as he referred to his agreed upon monthly amount, remained consistent each month just like mine, regardless of the pay for that period. Somehow, his brilliant revelation suggested to him that in the good months, his allowance should be reflective of his pay. After all, that would be fair. The more he made should increase his allowance. Brilliant, right? However, under our current compromise, he received the same amount, even when he brought in significantly more pay to our budget. That just didn't seem fair.

If you want your marriage to last and you find yourself in a similar situation, you have a choice. Divorce or compromise. Obviously our first compromise was not working nor was it fair, at least according to this revelation. Often, couples must figure out a way to make things work. Hence, we decided to work out another compromise.

I must admit, I do enjoy a little challenge now and then. And this compromise was a challenge in my mind – one that could easily end up in a battle in order to solve. We were definitely on opposite sides of this dilemma. If I am going to take the time to battle, I am not going to lose the battle. This battle proved to be a fun exercise in communication, at least for me.

Challenge accepted.

According to this brilliant revelation, based completely on logic, if my husband brought in more income certain months, his allowance would increase accordingly. Since my paycheck never varied, this did not affect anything for me. In the good months, shall we say, the allowance should increase. And he was ok if mine did too. We are married and it's all in one account.

I had no desire to increase my allowance from the original compromise. This just left his monthly allowance in question. I proposed the following as a new compromise. I would agree to increase his allowance accordingly in the months that he had a higher paycheck than average. But, in the months that his paycheck was lower than average, his allowance was zero. The choice was his.

Either compromise was acceptable to me. The original consistent allowance or the new and improved one based upon the brilliant revelation from his coworkers. It only took a few moments until the light bulb came on. My husband could continue to receive the same amount each month to use at his discretion, or he could receive an allowance based upon what he made that month. Can you guess what he chose? Yep, the original plan. What's even more incredible is that after 30 years together, that original plan is still in place.

We decided to include a similar process for expenses like our tax payments, insurance premiums, savings, and emergency fund. We moved money to a separate account designated for specific purposes that we both agreed to. That way, when the bill was due, we could just pay the bill since the money was in the account. There was no need to figure out how to pay the unexpected taxes. We just wrote the check and paid the bill.

Were there times when unexpected expenses arose that we didn't plan for? Of course. But it wasn't difficult to adjust the plan slightly to make up and adjust for those expenses. The best part is that it all starts with a basic budget, one that you review and adjust regularly.

To get you started, you can use this Basic Budget Template.

Basic Budget			
Month:			
		Planned	*Spent*
Income			
Expenses			
	Rent		
	Loans		
Credit Card Payments			
	Card 1		
	Card 2		
Other Expenses			
	Insurance		
	Taxes		
	Utilities		
	Phone		
	Internet		
	Professional Development		
	Advertising/Marketing		
	Other		
Giving			
	Donations		
Savings			
	Emergency Fund		
	Savings		
Grand Total			

Remember, a budget just provides direction for your money, so you don't have to wonder where your money went. You get to decide where your money is going ahead of time. You get to decide what expenses you are going to pay. You get to set aside money as it comes in so that you can pay certain expenses without stress. You get to repel Murphy at least, well, at the beginning of the month anyway.

Then at the end of the month you can compare your plan to the actual numbers. Now you can:

- Begin to make smarter decisions going forward.
- Adjust your budget accordingly to deal with the unexpected.

A budget allows you to start climbing that ladder of success. It makes sure that your ladder is leaning on the right building. The last thing you want to do is make it to the top and realize that you are on top of the "wrong" building. Without a budget, without a plan, without making time to review, your money may actually be on top of a different building and you wouldn't know it until you climbed the ladder and realized you were leaning your ladder against the wrong building.

Bite 4: Schedule a monthly meeting with yourself to review your reports

"The distance between dreams and reality is called action."

~Unknown.

If you are working through the process outlined, you have now taken at least three bites towards eating your elephant, Money. You separated your personal and business accounts, you have a system in place to track your income and expenses, and you have a budget. Now is the time to set up a system to create and review those key financial reports necessary for financial stability.

First, you need to be able to produce key reports. The key reports are the profit and loss statement, balance sheet, and a cash flow statement. If you are using a software program, these reports are built into the program. You just need to click a few buttons. If you are not using a program, you will have to create them in the spreadsheet or manually.

Once you have these reports, you need to review and analyze them so that you can determine if you are going in the direction you desire. The only way to do this is to schedule a monthly meeting. Yes, a monthly meeting with yourself.

Schedule it now. Pick a day and time and put it on your calendar. Treat it like a doctor's appointment. Treat it like you would the most valuable client. Schedule it each month and block off time on your calendar to pull these reports and study them. Your success depends on it.

If you were getting ready to go on your dream vacation, would you agree that taking the time to review your packing checklist would ensure you didn't forget something important? Or would you be so excited that you'd just pack your bags and head to the airport without double checking the list because it really wasn't that important?

This scheduled meeting allows you to determine your financial goals. When you have a goal, you have a direction. When you have a direction, you can manage your money to meet that goal. Blocking off time to review and analyze your numbers will make it possible for you to take control of your money, so that you can achieve that goal.

It forces you to be accountable for how your money flows in and out of your business. When you are accountable and take control of your money, you can pay your team, pay yourself, and pay your bills in a timely manner.

This monthly meeting can reveal anomalies you may not realize need to be changed. Once you realize it, you can take the necessary actions to rectify and plan for the desired future results. If successful entrepreneurs make the time, don't you think you should too?

There is one more critical aspect of your scheduled monthly meeting, the reconciliation process. A reconciliation is simply comparing your bank statement to your checkbook. Whether you use software or not, it is important to compare the transactions that the bank processed to your transactions in your financial system.

Although it may seem redundant, it's important to compare the two. Why? Maybe your $25 check was incorrectly processed as $250 by the bank. Maybe that $500 payment you're expecting from your client was inadvertently processed to someone else's bank account.

If you are certain that you or your bank will never inadvertently make an error, then don't worry about the reconciliation process. However, if you understand that errors happen and mistakes are made, often inadvertently, then the reconciliation process is vital. It's the only way you are going to discover that the error occurred. When you realize the error, you can correct it in a timely manner.

The same holds true for credit cards. Take the time each month to review the charges on your credit card. Too often automated charges are paid month after month, even after you canceled the service. Too often fraudulent charges hit your account.

If you don't review your credit card statements, you may be paying more than you are responsible for.

Bite 5: Squash the debt monster

"If you are willing to live like no one else, you can live like no one else."

~ Dave Ramsey

It's no surprise that credit cards can be a major contributor to expenses getting out of control. The more you use credit cards without paying them off, the higher your debt becomes. Soon the debt is like a monster consuming all the income you bring in and more. Soon things get out of control and you are back on that hamster wheel.

If this is the case, then you must take radical measures to get it under control. You must be willing to cut up credit cards until it is under control. Yes, cut up your credit cards.

As I start working with new clients, I take a close look at the credit card statement. For one client, this proved to be very revealing as to why he was struggling so much financially. When we reviewed the charges for the past several statements and totaled all the categories, what he thought he was spending each month on his credit card proved to be five times more than that. He didn't realize it because he was only paying the minimum amount due every month, without looking at the statement. As you can imagine, the balance never seemed to go down much.

What was even worse: Because he didn't realize how much he was spending, he also didn't realize how much interest he was paying just to use that credit card. That's a double whammy! And he wondered why he was struggling so much.

Suppose you wanted to carry water from one location to another. Would it make sense to use a container with holes? Of course not. You would require a container without holes or at least plug the holes until you achieved your goal. It's the same when it comes to debt. To achieve your goals, you must plug or stop the expenses that are out of control. When your debt is out of control, your expenses are out of control and you will struggle financially. Plug the holes, eliminate the debt, and get it under control.

I am not against having credit cards, as they can be convenient, and I have a couple myself. However, I pay them off each month without hesitation. They are there if I need the funds, but I don't use them without having a plan to pay the full balance that month or within two months at most.

Choose to take control of your debt, even if it takes a little time to get it under control. Start by writing down all your debt, including all your outstanding balances on your credit cards from lowest to highest. Only then will you see the true reality of your debt.

Now make a plan to start reducing your debt, one debt at a time. Dave Ramsey suggests using the "Debt Snowball"[14] to get your debt under control. In essence, you start by paying only the minimum amounts for each outstanding debt item. Then you pay as much as you possibly can to the lowest debt balance. Continue this process until you eliminate each debt item from your list. Of course, you cannot add any more debt until you get your current debt under control. If you are willing to be diligent and commit this process, you can get your debt monster under control.

Just like those little expenses add up, your debt reduction adds up. The difference this time is that you are in control.

Let's figure out where you are at this point, so you have a starting point. Identify the following for a typical month. Most

Debt Starting Point		
Monthly	**Debt & Expenses**	
Recurring Monthly Expenses		
	Rent	
	Loans	
Credit Card Payments		
	Card 1	
	Card 2	
Other Expenses		
	Insurance	
	Taxes	
	Utilities	
	Phone	
	Internet	
	Professional Development	
	Advertising/Marketing	
	Other	
Grand Total		

likely there will be other items. You can download the Debt Template and adjust as needed from your toolkit.

Bite 6: Be proactive not reactive

"The secret to change is to focus all your energy not on fighting the old, but on building the new."

~Socrates

In order to make sure that you have the money available to pay upcoming expenses, it requires you to be proactive, not reactive. When it comes to money, being proactive means that you will need to set money aside ahead of time or allocate it prior to paying the expense.

In other words, as money comes into your account, you allocate or move money out of your main account to another one. You only pay specific expenses from this separate account. To be successful, you must allocate money before it is spent. Specific expenses such as taxes and insurance premiums are great examples. That way, when the bill comes in, the money is available to pay the bill.

This is known as the allocation system, which can be enhanced as time goes on. But for now, let's focus only on the following expenses: taxes and insurance premiums. These are expenses that you know are coming up eventually, but not immediately. Over time, you can expand the allocation process to include your pay and even a profit allocation. But for now, let's start with the two expenses above.

First, set up a secondary checking account, separate from your main operating account. It will only be used for the two identified expenses above at this time. The process requires you to move money ahead of time in a consistent manner to cover these two expenses.

How it works: you can start with a bi-monthly allocation (twice per month). As income is received, you use an allocation template to determine the amount to move to the separate account. Then you move that amount twice a month to the separate account. Before you make any additional buying decisions, make sure you have allocated this amount. Once allocated, you can determine what money is left to work with.

Let's start with the insurance premium. What is the total yearly insurance premium amount? Divide the total by 24 if you have 12 months left before the premium is due. You may have to make a little adjustment if you don't have 12 months to work with prior to the due date. For this example, let's assume you have 12 months.

- Example: Your premium is $1,200.
- Divide the $1,200 by 24 (12 months, split up and allocated twice a month equals 24).
- Result: the allocation for this expense is $100 per month; $50 per allocation.

You will move, on a bi-monthly basis, $50 to cover the expense that is due in 12 months.

Now, let's figure out an allocation for taxes. This one needs a little extra math to figure out.

For simplicity, let's assume that you pay 15% of your income in taxes. Remember, we are simply starting to build the process. It's more important to understand the concept rather than figure out the exact percent at this time. Yes, you will need to figure it out, but your accountant can help with that. You can make adjustments later. Right now, focus on the process. There are resources and tools available to you www.janetIckes.com/Resources to guide your process. For this example, let's make the following assumption:

- Example: Your income is $1,000.
- Taxes are 15%: multiply $1,000 by 15%.
- Result: Tax allocation is $150.

Now, schedule the allocation or transfer to move $200 to the separate account.

- $50 for insurance
- $150 for taxes

Consistency is the key. Income comes in and you allocate it according to your plan. Even better, you can start to move your pay and profit over to this account as well.

Once completely in place, this process allows you to, on occasion, make a buying decision based upon the amount in your operating account. You already allocated the "spent" amounts as part of your process. So technically, the amount left has to cover all other expenses.

It will be better to make a decision about whether or not you could afford "this or that" using this process, especially if you are prone to check your checking account before saying "yes."

Bite 7: Streamline and document your processes

"Life is really simple, but we insist on making it complicated."

~ Confucius

Have you ever found yourself doing things the "hard way?" Ever get that awesome new present, the one that states that assembly is required? Then when you pull out the instructions, you find that there are at least 100 steps just to get all the pieces put together. Often, we perform a lot of little steps just to get our desired results. You find yourself wondering and hoping that there is a better way, a faster way, a simpler way.

Processes are a natural part of life. You do them without even thinking about many of them. Do you put the mail in the same place so you can make sure the bills are not misplaced? Do you put your keys in the same place so that tomorrow you can grab them and leave on time? Do you go the same way to work every day? Many will answer "yes" to these questions.

Often these processes or workflows turn into habits. Habits can be good and some not so good. The bottom line is to determine if the steps you are taking to achieve the desired result have become good or bad habits. Habits still need to be evaluated. Often there is a better way, but it's just a habit to keep doing it the same way. Too often you fail to take a look at the process to determine if there is a better way available.

This bite starts by documenting your processes. Document the process when you add a new client. Document the process for the payment process. You get the idea. All areas of your business should have documentation to support the tasks, especially the repetitive ones.

Once documented, you can review the process periodically, such as quarterly or yearly to determine if there may be a better, more streamlined way to complete the tasks at hand. You must take a step back and determine if the process is worth the exchange of time and money for the result that you expect. This review is especially true with money management.

What are the steps that you are taking to make sure you are recording your income and expenses consistently? Are you manually writing down each transaction in detail? Are you utilizing a software program that automates some of those mundane tasks?

If you invest in the software, are you using that software to its fullest potential? Odds are, you are not. Most people only use about 20% of a software's potential. Why? It may be because they don't realize what the software is capable of. Or maybe they don't understand the software. Maybe it is because they are content with the current process, even if it takes 25 times as long to achieve the goal; at least the goal was met.

What is your process to receive customer payments? What steps do you take? What information do you need? More than likely, it's the same for each client. Document the process. Is the process manual or is it automated? Maybe when you evaluate the process, you can add one step that will automate the process and make it run just a little more efficiently.

So often, there are ways to automate, but if you are continually trying to figure out the process because you didn't document it, you will never be able to take the time to figure out a different way. You may be able to utilize software, but if it's set up improperly because you are unsure of the ultimate outcome and specifics steps, software can end up costing you more time, energy, and money.

Processes save us time or take over our time. Processes can be complicated or simple. When you set up your process flow properly, you can achieve greater results. In order to achieve better results, you have to review them and streamline them as opportunities arise. Streamlining documented processes leads to more efficient ways to accomplish the same goals. More efficiency leads to more profits. More profits lead to a higher paycheck. You have the choice. Choose to work smarter, not harder.

Work smarter, not harder!

Bite 8: Determine your strengths and delegate

"Deciding what not to do is as important as deciding what to do."

~ Jessica Jackley

As an entrepreneur, I suspect that you have pretty good idea of what your strengths are when it comes to business. Most likely, you are good at the service you provide. However, you may not be so good at the details required to maintain solid accounting records. By now, you realize these are essential if you plan to stay in business very long.

When you determine your strengths, you can focus on them. Use them to grow and support your business. Finances are crucial and you must have an understanding of them. Yes, you have to know how money is flowing in and out of your business, but do you absolutely have to know each and every transaction? Maybe details are not your strength. What can you do? You can delegate certain tasks to someone else who has that as their strength.

Have you ever found yourself driving down the highway and suddenly you realize you have a flat tire? You could change the tire, or you could simply call roadside assistance.

Delegation is a key to your success. There are only 24 hours in a day, and sometimes it seems like we have 72 hours of work to get done each and every day. Take a close look at successful entrepreneurs; they are most likely master delegators. They know that it is vital to focus on activities that bring income into the business. They know that it's important to manage the cash that flows in and out of the business. But does that mean that they have to be the one taking care of every transaction? Does it mean that they must be an expert on tax laws? Does it mean that they must understand exactly how debits and credits work, so that they can manually enter every transaction? No!

In fact, there is no way one person can take care of it all. To succeed, you must have support. You must find support for those areas, especially in the areas you're not capable of handling yourself. Support is vital and you have to be able and willing to delegate to be successful.

Processes have to be documented so that they can be followed. That way, when something doesn't work as expected, you can figure out what needs to change. Surround yourself with those who complement your strengths and pay them well to use their strengths to help and support you and your business. They are worth their weight in gold when it comes to running a successful business. The same applies when it comes to money.

If you are not able to keep up with the ever-changing tax laws, invest in an accountant to prepare your taxes. If coding transactions drive you nuts, invest in a bookkeeper to manage the transactions as they flow in and out of your bank account.

Delegate the tasks but understand the big picture. After all, it's up to you, not them, to run your business.

As you take one bite at a time, remember the choice is yours. It is up to you.

We have covered eight bites that will give you a start to build your solid financial foundation on rock. Each bite propels you one step forward.

And starting with this simple system is only effective if properly implemented and used. The solution is possible, and with a little guidance and direction you can take control of where your money goes.

I have used the systems explained for both my personal and business finances. I want to inspire you to take one bite, just one bite. One bite will take you closer to being able to manage your money. That's why I wrote this book. It's by design and it provides a foundation for financial success. Ignite the possibilities in your business and in your personal finances. Ignite the passion to understand money so that you can control how it flows in and out of your life. When you plan and proactively take control of your finances, money gives you choices. So take one bite at time.

Yes, each bite requires a system; each bite takes commitment.

- Commitment each and every day.
- Commitment to make the tough decisions.
- Commitment to think before you buy.
- Commitment to set aside a few dollars each month to deal with those unexpected expenses.

Is it easy? No, it's simple. Each bite gets you closer.

- Closer to managing your money.
- Closer to reducing your stress from trying to figure out how you are going to pay your expenses.

- Closer to making better decisions to support your financial goals.

Each and every bite makes a difference.

Every bite:

- Can be applied to either your personal or business finances to build the foundation necessary to sustain wealth.
- Eliminates the excuses holding you back.
- Allows you to choose to face challenges as opportunities. And we know life is full of challenges, and life is busy.
- Moves you one step closer to your desired results.
- Slows the hamster wheel down just a little bit.
- Gets you closer to the flexibility and financial freedom your business is supposed to provide.

You started your business because you have a solution that will help others. You wanted to have flexibility and freedom that owning your own business provides. Yes, there are two sides to owning your own business. There is the freedom side, and there is the risk side. Both are part of owning your own business. Business includes risk. Yet, with proper planning, strategies, and execution, you can set your business up for success one bite at a time. You can weather the storms that arise. You can choose to build that foundation on rock, so that you enjoy the benefits of owning your own business. You can choose to enjoy a life with less stress because you know where your money is. And you have a plan to manage it.

Each bite helps you to determine how much income you need to cover expenses and how close your expectations come to your reality. If you want long-term success, each bite helps you to figure out what you need to know, what you need to change, and what you need to continue because it works. Knowing your numbers is the key. You must track your numbers.

There are a few numbers in business that you have to know. You have to know these numbers if you want long-term success. And the bites will build the foundation necessary to identify these numbers.

Numbers you need to know:

- How much money do you earn, aka, what is your monthly income?
- What are your monthly expenses?
- What expenses do you owe?
- When are those expenses due?
- What is left over each month?

Each bite enables you to answer these questions. Answers to these questions lead you towards your ultimate goals and lifestyle. But it all starts with you. It starts with the choice to take control of your money. Why? Because money doesn't spend itself.

A Time to Reflect

Question #3: What can I do right now?

"If you fail to plan, you are planning to fail." ~ Benjamin Franklin

Track your progress: Check off what you have accomplished.

✓ Separate business and personal accounts

✓ System in place to track income and expenses

- What system are you using? ____________________

✓ Budget is created

- What system are you using? ____________________

✓ Monthly Meeting is scheduled

- What is the date and time of this meeting? _______

✓ System is set up to allocate income to expense accounts before expenses are paid

- How often do you allocate income? _____________
- What is the process?__________________________

✓ Processes are documented and reviewed to streamline

What can you do differently in the future?

____

____

____

Identify three areas that you can delegate and who you can delegate them to.

____________________ to who ____________________

____________________ to who ____________________

____________________ to who ____________________

Inspirational Thought:

In all your ways acknowledge him and he will direct your path. ~ Proverbs 3:6 (ESV)

Notes/Thoughts

Chapter 5

Money Doesn't Spend Itself.

"A dream witten down with a date becomes a Goal. A goal broken down into steps becomes a Plan. A plan backed by Action makes your dreams come true"

~ Greg Reid

Let's recap. We know that money doesn't spend itself, so where did it go?

Question 1: Where is my money? It's not in my account.

Step 1. Figure out where the money went. Remember it can be as simple as picking up a piece of paper and a pen. Combined with a little addition and subtraction, you can figure out where your money is, especially if it's not in your account.

Write down all your income received during the month as well as all the expenses for the month. Yes, all income and expenses. You must track every penny, every nickel, every dollar. It's the only way to figure out where your money is. It's the only way to figure out at the end of the month, what you earned. It's the only way to figure out if you had a profit or a loss.

Get a total amount for your income and expenses. In other words, add up all income together and all expenses together for a grand total. Now, subtract the expenses from the income. Is the number positive or negative?

Confused yet?

Let's make it simple:

> My total income for the month is: _______________
>
> My total expenses for the month are: ____________

Now for the hard part:

> Subtract your expenses from your income and enter the total here: ______________________________

What did your number show? Is the number positive or negative? Just in case you were wondering, you want it to be positive. If this number is not greater than zero, you need to make some adjustments, now.

Tracking is the only way you can figure out if you were profitable and your income was greater than your expenses.

What if you were not profitable? What can you do? You only have a couple of choices. You can either increase your income or decrease your expenses. By tracking each transaction, at least you will know the value of your expenses and amount of income. Tracking makes it possible to make smarter decisions based on numbers, not emotion, and decide what options you really have to increase your income and decrease your expenses.

Question 2:
What happens when it all breaks loose?

Step 2. Plan.

Without a plan, you have no direction, and without a direction you will end up exhausted, running on a hamster wheel that you will never be able to get off of, until you fall off. Without a plan, you will have no idea what happens when it all breaks loose. Without a plan, you cannot set aside funds to buffer and repel Murphy and Mayhem. Without a plan, you cannot face a typical day, let alone be able to respond. You will only be able to react. Your stress will increase, putting your health, your business, and your family at risk.

Question 3:
Where do you start?

Step 3. Take the first bite, then one bite at time. Take the first step, then one step at a time.

Where do you start? You start by eating the elephant, Money. How do you eat an elephant? One bite at a time. Just like a toddler learning to walk. As parents, it seems like one day they are crawling and the next they are running; the reality is that first they sit up. They crawl. Then they try to stand. They fall. They sit back up. Maybe crawl a little more. They try to stand and eventually they are strong enough to take a step. They fall. And the process repeats. And before long they are not just standing, not just walking, but they are running. The same holds true for you when it comes to money. You have to sit before you crawl. You have to crawl before you walk, and you have to walk before you run. Yes, you will fall, but with each fall you get back up, stronger than before. You are stronger and able to take one more step, one step at a time. If you fall, get back up and take another step.

Action leads to success. One step at a time will get you where you are going. One bite at a time will allow you to eventually eat the elephant. Don't give up! Just get up and take the next step. Don't think about it; just do it. If doing it requires getting support, find support. Get help and even delegate. Delegate the tracking of those annoying transactions to a bookkeeper. Invest in a good accountant who will keep you tax compliant. Invest in a system that will help streamline the necessary steps to record and summarize your income and expenses. Invest in training from an expert who can help you design a system that you will use to make managing your money simple.

Track your progress on your path:

- Separate business and personal accounts
- System in place to track income and expenses
- Create and use a budget
- Schedule a monthly meeting and review your key financial reports
- Set up a plan to reduce debt to a manageable level
- Set up a system to allocate income to a separate account before it's spent
- Document and review your systems and processes
- Determine what tasks can be delegated and delegate them

As you check these off the items above, know that you are building a foundation on rock. A foundation that will withstand challenges and unexpected financial obligations.

Even better, track your progression over the next 12 months…

Let's see the progression				
Check if the answer is "YES"	**Today's Date: ______**	**3 Months: ______**	**6 Months: ______**	**12 Months: ______**
Do you have separate business/personal accounts?				
Do you have a system in place to track your income and expenses?				
Do you have a budget in place?				
Do you use that budget monthly?				
Do you have your monthly meeting on your calendar?				
Do you have a system set up to allocation income before you spend it?				
Do you have your processes documented?				
Name 3 Tasks you can delegate and note when you are able to delegate them				
1				
2				
3				
Did you review your processes?	______			
Do you have plan in place to manage debt?				

Focus on your strengths and get help or delegate the areas that are not producing income. This way you can focus on the ones that are, the ones that improve and support your growth. Delegate the tasks you simply don't like to do to someone who has a strength in that area.

Understand where your money is and how your money flows in and out of your account. This understanding is vital to your success. Knowing how the money flows through your business is vital to the longevity of your business. The same principles hold true in your personal finances. The way you manage your personal finances will mirror in your business finances.

The responsibility is yours. You have a choice. Money doesn't spend itself.

Progress is based on consistency. There will be challenges. There will be good months and not so good months. It's expected. It's life. But the key to success and building a solid foundation is consistency, even if it's only one baby step or one bite at a time.

And when you get a handle on where your money is, you can take responsibility for it. You can make sure it's in your account. When it's in your account, you can tell it where to go.

Imagine how it would feel:

- to pay your bills without stress.
- to know that your business will provide a paycheck that will support your lifestyle.
- to know where your money is.
- to know that those unexpected expenses are really expected, and you have savings to cover them.
- to not find yourself in a financial crisis if you need $400 dollars to cover an expense.

- to know that if you have to deal with an emergency, you have at least $1,000 set aside to repel Murphy and Mayhem.

Imagine how it would feel if you weren't stressed when it comes to money. When you are less stressed, you worry less, you yell less, your family dynamics would ultimately improve, and you would be able to enjoy the freedom of owning your own business. You would know that your business will provide financial stability for you and your family. Isn't that why you opened your own business in the first place?

Even if you are not good at numbers, if you can understand them, you can take control of your money. You can implement a system that helps manage the details.

You started with a dream, a dream to own your own business. You had a goal to grow that business and enjoy the flexibility that owning your own business offers. Now are you ready to take one bite at a time – to track, to plan, and to take action to achieve the dream you started with.

Are you willing? Are you willing to make the necessary changes to figure out where your money is? Is it worth it? Is it:

- Worth being less stressed?
- Worth having a healthier lifestyle that is not consumed by stress?
- Worth being able to get a good night's sleep because you are not worried over whether or not you can pay your bills or pay yourself?
- Worth knowing that your business will be able to provide a paycheck that will support your personal lifestyle?

Only you can answer if it is worth it.

Yes, the process may seem overwhelming. Yes, there is work involved. Yes, you have to make some hard choices. But you can take one bite at a time, one step at time. You can reach out to experts who can help you.

Remember the story, "The Tortoise and The Hare?" The hare is confident of winning, so it is willing to stop during the race. It falls asleep. The tortoise continues to move, very slowly, one step at a time, without stopping. The result: the tortoise wins the race! Slow and steady will win the race. Every bite, every step, even a baby step gets you closer to the finish line. One bite, one step, one change at a time, will make all the difference. If you are willing to figure out where your money is, you can make a plan for what happens when it all breaks lose. With a plan in place, you can begin to take one bite, without burning out before the finish line. Choose to take that bite, that step forward until you achieve your goal. Have faith that you can do it. Have faith that you can take control of your money. After all, it wasn't raining when Noah built the Ark, and money doesn't spend itself!

Chapter 6

Where Do I Go From Here?

Drive the car but look in the mirror along the way. Great leaders pave the way for others. They drive the car. But great leaders also look in the mirror. When you drive a car, you must be watching and scanning out the windshield in order to reach your destination. You must continually be looking for obstacles and be willing and able to go around them. Looking ahead, through the windshield, keeps you focused on where you want to go.

At the same time, unless you also look in the side mirrors and rear-view mirror, you are setting yourself up to fall short of making it to your intended destination. You must know what is beside and behind you. Only then can you find ways to maneuver around others. Only then can you avoid a potentially dangerous driver who is weaving through traffic behind you.

If you are aware of what is on all sides, you'll have a good opportunity to avoid an accident. You will be able to respond instead of react to the drivers in front, beside, and behind you.

It's no different when it comes to money. You have to know your goals and how much money you need to achieve them. You have to know your expenses so that you can be prepared to pay them. You have to know that you are profitable so that you can get paid. You have to get paid if you are in business.

Look through the windshield and see the future. Look in the rear-view mirror to see the progress. Take the necessary steps and arrive at the destination of your choice.

Don't forget to take advantage of my Special Bonus Gift

There's so much information out there about money management that can help you to run a profitable business, yet at the same time, it can be very confusing. Now that you've finished this book, you're armed with what you need to know to build a foundation that will sustain future growth so that you can successfully manage your money. It's a great place to get started so that you can reduce hours researching and instead focus more on what really matters.

As a special bonus for buying this book, I've created templates to help you get started with getting your arms around your business finances. It's the *Know Where Your Money Is Toolkit,* filled with downloadable templates to get you started tracking your income and expenses and creating a budget, as well as checklists to help you stay focused and on task with primary financial activities.

As an additional bonus, you'll also have access to a resource page with links to not only the resources mentioned in this book, but also to new tools, technologies, and programs I discover and recommend.

Just go to https://JanetIckes.com/MoneyToolKit and let me know where to send your bonus kit.

As another special gift, I'll also be sending tips, tricks, and great information to make your life easier around your business finances.

Let's continue the momentum!

Janet

About the Author

Over a 20-year corporate career in the accounting and payroll fields, Janet Ickes developed a broad knowledge and expertise in financial management and budgeting. Holding roles as Finance Manager, Senior Accountant, and AVP of Payroll in both the oil and gas industry and banking provided vast opportunities to train, learn, and grow both professionally and personally. She now brings this expertise and wisdom to entrepreneurs and small business owners who want to grow a thriving business.

Through her direct, yet calm, hands-on training approach, she encourages creative options within the system boundaries that meet the needs of those she works with.

Alongside her corporate career, she inspires others to put their best face forward as an Independent Mary Kay Beauty Consultant. For over 20 years, through skin care education and consultations, she continues to inspire others to put their best face forward confidently.

After leaving her corporate career, Janet and her family moved from Pennsylvania to North Carolina. Initially, the plan was to grow her part time-time Mary Kay business into a full-time one. However, the Lord had a little different plan that unveiled as she grew her Mary Kay business.

Blending her corporate and small business experience and expertise, she launched **Excel with Me Training and Consulting, LLC**. She realized that she could share her expertise, from corporate to small business owners. Her varied background, along with her unique training approach allows her clients to build financially stable businesses, focused on growing profits and utilizing systems to their fullest potential. She inspires those she works with and ignites possibilities as she works with her clients to find ways to work smarter, not harder.

Acknowledgements

First and foremost, I want to thank the Lord for granting me the privilege to write this book. He has placed so many in my path that have helped me to become who I am today. It's been an amazing journey so far and I am so grateful for all those that the Lord has placed alongside me, in front of me, and behind me. Whether they were to challenge me, support me, knock me down, or lift me back up, their touch on my life contributed to this book.

I want to thank my family, especially my husband Tim, for always standing beside me no matter what. We have been together 30 years and I am so thankful that the Lord provided such a wonderful man to share my journey with. There have been so many good times and, of course, a few challenging ones. But I never doubted your love and support, and I know that no matter what we face, we will face it together.

Thank you to my son Kyle, whose infinite teenage wisdom proves to be challenging and rewarding at the same time. We often take one step forward and 16 back. But I know that one way or another, we will figure it out. You continually challenge me to be the best I can be.

Thank you to my parents, Hazel and Glenn Riddell, for providing such a phenomenal foundation, especially when it comes to money management. They waited 20 years for my arrival and had just about given up all hope. But they should have known that God had a plan, one that was in His time and included a sense of humor. Happy April Fool's Day! Today you become parents (and He was not kidding).

I have been so blessed by the many who have crossed my path. So many friends have supported me, strengthened me, and even carried me when I couldn't walk.

Thank you to Diana M. Needham, whose guidance has truly been a blessing as you challenged me to be better, challenged my writing, and challenged me each step of the way. It's the challenges that make us stronger. Thank you for your wisdom and guidance through this process. I am incredibly grateful you are my friend, for this book would not be what is today without you.

So many business mentors and coaches have helped me along the way. They focused my thoughts, challenged me, guided me, helped me, and even blocked me when needed. Together, they encouraged me to go beyond what I thought was possible. They urged me to figure it out and move forward, no matter what obstacles were in the way. They offered their wisdom without reservation, guiding and shaping my path so that I could succeed. And I am so grateful.

And I thank you, the courageous entrepreneur who is ready and willing to build a financially stable business, one bite at a time.

Notes on Sources

Chapter 1

1. US Bank Study, Business Insider (August 2017); https://www.businessinsider.com/why-small-businesses-fail-infographic-2017-8?r=US&IR=T>
2. The Associated Press-NORC Center for Public Affairs Research, US News, 8 Scary Financial Statistics-and How to Avoid Becoming One (May 2017); https://money.usnews.com/money/personal-finance/saving-budget/articles/2017-05-16/8-scary-financial-statistics-and-how-to-avoid-becoming-one
3. FINRA's National Financial Capability Study, US News, 8 Scary Financial Statistics-and How to Avoid Becoming One, (May 2017); https://money.usnews.com/money/personal-finance/saving-budget/articles/2017-05-16/8-scary-financial-statistics-and-how-to-avoid-becoming-one
4. Survey of Consumer Finances, US Federal Reserve Debt Facts *#92*; https://www.moneysavedmoneyearned.com/101-fascinating-money-facts/
5. Bureau of Labor Statistics Business Employment Dynamics, Fundara What Percentage of Small Businesses Fail? (And Other need-to-Know Stats), (July 2020); https://www.fundera.com/blog/what-percentage-of-small-businesses-fail
6. Money Saved Is Money Earned, 101 Fascinating Money Facts, Tawnya Redding; https://www.moneysavedmoneyearned.com/101-fascinating-money-facts

Chapter 2

7. Association of Young Americans (AYA) and AARP, Best Money Moves), What percentage of Americans Spend More than They Earn? (October 2018); https://bestmoneymoves.com/blog/2018/10/03/what-percentage-of-americans-spend-more-than-they-earn/

Chapter 3

8. The Associate Press-NORC Center for Public Affairs Research, The Associated Press Poll (May 2016); https://apnews.com/965e48ed609245539ed315f83e01b6a2
9. 2018 Survey of Household Economics and Decision Making Report, Report on Economic Well Being of US Households in 2018 (May 2019); https://www.federalreserve.gov/publications/2019-economic-well-being-of-us-households-in-2018-dealing-with-unexpected-expenses.htm
10. CNN Money Special Report Issue #1 America's Money Crisis; (January 2009); https://money.cnn.com/2009/01/15/real_estate/millions_in_foreclosure/#:~:text=NEW%20YORK%20(CNNMoney.com),its%20year%2Dend%20report%20Thursday
11. RealtyTrack, CNN Money Special Report Issue #1 America's Money Crisis (January 2009); https://money.cnn.com/2009/01/15/real_estate/millions_in_foreclosure/#:~:text=NEW%20YORK%20(CNNMoney.com),its%20year%2Dend%20report%20Thursday
12. Credit Donkey, 23 Dizzying Average American Savings Statistics, Rebecca Lake (February 2020) https://www.creditdonkey.com/average-american-savings-statistics.html

Chapter 4

13. US Bank Possibility Index, US Bank Study, CNN Money, Nearly 3 in 5 Americans are making this huge financial mistake, Maurie Backmon (October 2016); https://money.cnn.com/2016/10/24/pf/financial-mistake-budget/index.html

14. Dave Ramsey Financial Peace Course, https://www.daveramsey.com/

Made in the USA
Columbia, SC
30 October 2020

23655604R00089